Making it Through the Dark Night of the Soul

Reverend Dr. Herman Brooks

Ordained Minister of the
United Centers for Spiritual Living
And
American Board Certified Psychiatrist

America Star Books
Frederick, Maryland

First printing

America Star Books has allowed this work to remain exactly as the author intended, verbatim, without editorial input.

This publication contains the opinions and ideas of its author. Author intends to offer information of a general nature. Any reliance on the information herein is at the reader's own discretion.

The author and publisher specifically disclaim all responsibility for any liability, loss, or right, personal or otherwise, which is incurred as a consequence, directly or indirectly, of the use and application of any contents of this book. They further make no representations or warranties with respect to the accuracy or completeness of the contents of this work and specifically disclaim all warranties including without limitation any implied warranty of fitness for a particular purpose. Any recommendations are made without any guarantee on the part of the author or the publisher.

Hardcover 9781682909225
Softcover 9781682903179
PUBLISHED BY AMERICA STAR BOOKS, LLLP
www.americastarbooks.pub
Frederick, Maryland

DEDICATION

To my beloved mother, Eloise Reed, whose memory I cherish and whose love and wisdom have been guideposts for my life.

And to Marion Falconbridge, also affectionately known as "Gita," who was the love of my life and who, before her passing, served as a catalyst and compass propelling me along my spiritual path.

ACKNOWLEDGMENTS

I would like to express my love and gratitude to the following people:

Eloise Reed, my beloved mother, whose memory I deeply cherish and who served as a source of inspiration throughout my life by consistently letting me know that I was loved and could be anything that I wanted to be.

Reverend Dr. Michael Bernard Beckwith, the Senior Minister and Founder of the Agape International Center of Truth in Culver City, California, who directed the foundation classes which I initially took in spiritual laws and principles and under whose tutorage I initially obtained my call to become a minister in the United Church of Religious Science now known as the United Centers for Spiritual Living.

Reverend Dr. Sage Bennett, former Dean and Director of the Holmes Institute School of Ministry, who was one of my instructors during my training. After reading one of my papers, she informed me that it was very good and suggested that I submit it for publishing. I sent the paper to the Science of Mind magazine. It was read, accepted, and subsequently published in the September 2002 edition and served as the catalyst to writing *Making it Through the Dark Night of the Soul.*

Alma Collins, a friend of more than 20 years, who has faithfully supported me socially and professionally in my private practice as a psychiatrist and as I matriculated through ministerial school. Without her support, my book would not have been possible.

Mary Yanish, one of the most significant relationships of my entire life, who introduced me to Catholic Mysticism when she gave me the book "Practicing the Presence of God," and who was instrumental in acquainting me with St. John of the Cross and his noted work, *The Dark Night of the Soul.*

Aurora Le Mere, a friend and educator, who has graciously lent her skills and services to help to perfect my work and make it as presentable, literate, and transformative as possible.

Fred Atkinson, Beverly Ware, Gail Edwards, Randall Klarin, Bufort McClerkins, Barbara Williams, and Shanti Bolden, who have all encouraged and supported me as I have traveled along my journey.

INTRODUCTION

MAKING IT THROUGH THE DARK NIGHT OF THE SOUL

St. John of the Cross, the author of the historic work *Dark Night of the Soul*, was a 16th century Catholic mystic. He lived in Spain and was a friar and priest of the Carmelite Order.

During his lifetime, he authored a number of works, many of which were beautiful and profound and influenced the thought of his period. Among his works was *The Ascent of Mt. Carmel*, which some religious scholars think may be his most important one. He was a spiritual master as well as a philosopher. The friar was a reformist of his order who sometimes fell into disfavor with his peers but who remained true to his divine purpose.

Although some may think other of his major works to be even more important, none can deny the lasting impact that his poem, "Dark Night of the Soul," and the subsequent analysis of it which formed the book of the same name, has had on the human psyche. The mere mention of the title conjures up deep felt images in the mind which may be attached to suffering or may be attached to transformation, sometimes both. In his writings, St. John of the Cross combined mysticism and philosophy and nowhere did he do it better than he did in his seminal work *Dark Night of the Soul* which has served to make an impression on humanity which has lasted for centuries.

I did not set out to write a book on the dark night. The book practically wrote itself. Initially, I wrote an article on stress which was published in the Science of Mind magazine. It came about as a result of a workshop which I had done entitled "Be Blessed Not Stressed." After putting the content of the workshop into a paper which I submitted to Reverend Sage Bennet, she liked it and was suitably impressed to suggest that it be submitted for publication. Following her direction, the paper was submitted, accepted, and subsequently published in the fall of 2002. One of my former patients happened to read the article and was moved by it. As he suffers from recurrent depressions, he asked if I would do a similar article on depressive episodes. The seed was planted.

Nothing came to me for years. After experiencing tragic events in my own life, including the passing of my mother, I became sufficiently refined to truly appreciate the effects of trauma and depression which enabled me to have a foundation upon which to write a work on depressive episodes. When I was finally inspired to transcribe it, what initially was meant to be a brief article continued to expand. More thoughts and ideas came regarding dealing with depression and spiritual turmoil until what was initially thought to be several pages became an entire book.

What served to cause the expansion were my own personal experiences and things which I observed during my fourteen years in private practice as a psychiatrist. Academics, knowledge gained in ministerial school, personal experiences, and professional experiences all served to make a brief discussion into the book which emerged.

The book itself is made up of three sections. The first segment consists of describing depressive episodes and the means by which to successfully overcome them. Maladaptive and dysfunctional mental habits are described in detail and habits which prolong depression are discussed. Psychological principles and adaptive practices such as certain tenets of cognitive behavioral therapy are discussed as well as medication and basic activities which promote, not only mental, but overall well-being are detailed. Cases of people with whom I have worked who used the means to actually overcome their own depressions are given and analyzed as examples of how one can overcome a severe depressive disorder.

The second section of the book is concerned with the spiritual component of the dark night. It makes the point that depression and the dark night of the soul are not one and the same. Although a depressive mood is part and parcel of the dark night, one can have profound depression and not be in the dark night. In order to be immersed in the darkness of the soul, one must have a spiritual component to his suffering. One must be moving through the shadow, which means ultimately there is a purging of his or her soul which is taking place and a transformation is at hand.

Spiritual practices and laws which can give one knowledge and the guidance to move towards the light are given in the middle segment, as well as a description of the process the spiritual seeker is to endure. A case study is once more given regarding a person who not only went through depression, but who also experienced moving through the shadow into the light as well. Also, I take from my own personal experiences during my private practice and my years of ministerial training to bring certain truths to the light for the use and benefit of the spiritual seeker who is going through the time of purgation.

In the first part of the book, there is an emphasis on psychological tools. In the second part, there is an emphasis on spiritual practices. It is also shown that, although overcoming depression will bring a person often to a more healthy state than he previously had, he still may not have been cleansed of any spiritual deficits. However, in overcoming the dark night, there is a purging, and one can move from being what St. John denotes as the state of a meditative into that of a contemplative through the process of purging by which one journeys from being a dilettante on the spiritual path to one who is committed to living a life rooted in God. When one truly completes the sensual part of the journey of the soul along the path through darkness, he gives himself in service to God and humanity. He finds the purpose for his life and is motivated to find union with God in love.

In the third part of the book, general comments are made regarding the metaphor of moving from shadow into light as being synonymous with moving from illness into well-being and from ignorance to a degree of understanding. Examples are given of great souls who have traversed the valley of shadow and an examination is done of all who are called unto the path of purgation.

Finally, concluding remarks are made regarding the changes which take place in overcoming depression, the purging and transformation which take place in moving from shadow into the light, and the promise at the end of the journey through the dark night of a deep and abiding, more perfect union with God in love.

CONTENTS

Chapter 1

THE NIGHT AND DESCENT OF DARKNESS

Origins of the concept of the dark night of the soul, it's meaning to humankind, and events which lead to darkness and depression.

The phrase "dark night of the soul" is one which has endured for more than four hundred years. There is something in it that brings forth imagery in the human psyche which is foreboding and fearful. At the same time, there is something about it which is intriguing and very mysterious as well. It conveys different meanings to different people, but regardless of one's culture or background, it penetrates into his inner being. It resonates with the fundamental vibration in the deep recesses of human consciousness. Images and feelings associated with the term vary from a dawning of the spirit to the deepest of depressions. Often, there is associated with the phrase the concept of intense inner turmoil which may be heartrending and excruciatingly painful.

Many people, when hearing the phrase, "dark night of the soul" think of a time of distress and despair. A depressed person, upon hearing it, may think of his or her own suffering with no hope of relief from his agony.

The phrase, "dark night of the soul" may have a different meaning to a spiritual seeker. Such a person may relate it to enduring a journey of transformation. It may be necessary to face a malevolent side of himself, and one may expect to be filled with remorse and regret but also with the possibility of redemption. In truth, all of the analogies and images are correct. Any one of them may describe a person, depending on his own level of spiritual development and awareness.

The phrase "dark night of the soul" was originally written by St. John of the Cross, a Catholic mystic, who lived in sixteenth century Spain. He became a Friar in the Carmelite Order and a priest. He has been described as the most sublime of all the Spanish mystics, and his writings are thought to be some of the greatest contributions to the literature of mysticism and true classics of spiritual literature. In the following verse, he eloquently described the method utilized by the soul in its journey along the spiritual road to attain a greater understanding of its union with God.

Stanzas of the Soul by St. John of the Cross

1. On a dark night, Kindled in love with yearnings – oh, Happy chance!
   I went forth without being observed, My house being now at rest.
2. In darkness and secure, By the secret ladder, Disguised – oh, happy chance!
3. In the happy night, In secret, when none saw me, Nor I beheld aught, Without light or guide, save That which burned in my heart.
4. This light guided me More surely than the light of noonday
   To the place where he (well I knew who!) was awaiting me –
   A place where none appeared.
5. Oh, night that guided, me, Oh, night more lovely than the dawn,
   Oh, night that joined Beloved with lover, Lover transformed in the Beloved!

6. Upon my flowery breast, Kept wholly for himself
     alone,
      There he stayed sleeping, and I caressed him, And
       The fanning of the cedars made a breeze.

7. The breeze blew from the turret As I parted his
     locks;
      With his gentle hand he wounded my neck. And
       Caused all senses to be suspended.

8. I remained, lost in oblivion; My face I reclined on
     the Beloved
      All ceased and I abandoned myself, Leaving my
       cares forgotten among the lilies.[1]

These stanzas of the poem are intended not only to describe the method followed by the soul in its journey towards a divine union with God but also to describe the properties which belong to the soul in pushing it to obtain perfection. The book *Dark Night of the Soul* is an in-depth literary expansion and exploration of the meaning of the stanzas written by the mystic, St. John of the Cross. Each chapter of the book is devoted to expounding at length upon the lines of the stanzas. Only a small part of the verse truly concerns itself with inner turmoil and agony which many of us think about when we consider the dark night of the soul. Most of the poem actually dwells on the joy and blessings which are received when we move forward into the light of spiritual transformation. Nonetheless, much of the book dwells on the first two verses which detail the spiritual and sensual purgation of a human being. The book, in its metaphysical analysis of the poem, helps one to go from the experience of a dark night of despair and uncertainty toward a dawn of faith and joyful illumination. A dark night of the soul can have numerous expressions.

Additionally, there are a number of events which can cause a "dark night of the soul" episode. In our human experience, a deep and abiding depression can be looked upon as being a dark night of the soul. A time of tragedy or crisis can be the triggering stressor which precipitates the emotional turmoil and brings it into manifestation. During the time of the dark night, there is intense personal trial and psychological conflict. A plunge into psychic battle is taking place and no one, not even the person experiencing it, can know the outcome. It is a unique experience, individual to each one who undergoes it, and it varies according to his perspective. What is common to all is that the journey affects each one at his innermost core. He is shaken at the very foundation of his being. Those who go through it are forever changed and transformed, never to be the same again.

When one thinks of the word "dark," he thinks of something which is without light. A dark time is a time that is hopeless and difficult to understand. Like the medieval dark ages, it is a time without enlightenment. A night is a period or condition of darkness. It is often a period of gloom and despair, a time of moral or intellectual degeneration and grief. It is the time of darkness after sunset and before sunrise. Metaphorically, it can symbolize the time in which one goes from ignorance to understanding, from damnation to transcendence.

The soul is the immortal or spiritual aspect of humankind. It is the spiritual and emotional essence of an individual. As souls, we are the individualized creative mediums of spirit. We experience things in our soul, which is the subjective side of our lives.

What we intuitively know and feel about the dark night of the soul is consistent with the meaning of it according to St. John of the Cross. He tells us that the meaning of dark is unseeing or hidden. It is more than simply a time of ignorance or turmoil. There is something about us that is unperceived during our time of trouble. Yes, the night may be associated with a time of grief or moral degeneration. It can be a time of gloom, but it is also a time of purging. It is analogous to the period of moving from the setting of the sun, or light, to a new dawning of awareness.

The soul itself embodies the spiritual and sensual sense of man. It is the essence of him as he journeys from the human side with its many failings to the perfection of the divine, for it is truly the divine with which mankind seeks union.

Psychologically, moving through the dark night of the soul in a mental sense is moving from a depressive state to one of well being. However, man is more than an intellect and an ego. In the full sense of the word, moving through the dark night of the soul from shadow to light means purgation. It means to make the soul of the seeker ready to receive union with God through love.

Indeed, the psychological difficulties must be challenged and overcome, but as one successfully deals with them, be it anxiety, depression or whatever may be the emotional context of the crisis, afterwards one must transcend to further transformation and growth. It is in this process that one moves from shadow to light and moves through the dark night of the soul. St. John of the Cross eloquently described the necessity of addressing one's spiritual and psychological deficits and accepting one's imperfection while yearning for and moving towards mental well being and spiritual perfection. "Into this dark night souls begin to enter when God draws them forth from the state of beginners, which is the state of those that meditate on the spiritual road, and begins to set them in the state of progressives, which is that of those who are already contemplatives to the end that after passing through it, they may arrive at the state of the perfect which is that of the divine union of the soul with God."[2]

There are a number of events which are associated with a severe depressive state and with the beginning of the dark night of the soul. Perhaps the one which is most common is grief. Grief is the powerful subjective emotion one feels following the death of a loved one. The more intimate and close one felt to the departed, the more intense and powerful the grief. We are often devastated when we lose a dear family member, close friend or even a beloved pet. We can be extremely depressed and moved into bereavement by the death of a parent.

Death is not the only thing which can push us into grieving. We can also grieve a failed relationship. Divorce can precipitate grief if one did not want the divorce and still desires the person who decided to no longer be a part of the union. One can even grieve the loss of a job. When someone's value and identification are intricately connected to the job that he had, the loss of being able to do the work and receive the rewards it brought can lead to a lasting depression.

Finally, we can even mourn the diminishing of our physical abilities. As we grow older, we are not able to do some activities that we could do when we were much younger. Oftentimes, we begin to have physical ailments which further diminish our abilities. Conditions such as arthritis, heart disease, and respiratory problems can reduce our ability to function, so we feel helpless and sometimes hopeless. All the identified losses can lead to grief, and ongoing grief can lead to depression and despair. Lasting despair can lead to significant depression. Examining the losses and trying to find meaning in what has happened can move one into the dark night of the soul.

During my career as a psychiatrist, I have had occasion to treat a number of people for depressive disorders. I have found that in order to deal with their spiritual turmoil, they also had to deal with their clinical depression. The psychological and the spiritual were intertwined and one could not move through the spiritual without first traversing the psychological.

One case in particular comes to mind. A client who I will call Mrs. C was brought to me by her family. She was a 58-year old widowed African-American, a petite female with three adult children. Until recently, she had been a very active woman in good health and well-being. Mrs. C worked for the telephone company and was generally very much liked by her colleagues and loved by her family. She was only 15 years of age when she first met her husband of 30 years who died unexpectedly in their home six weeks before my meeting with her. She was the one who discovered his body. Throughout their long marriage, she had been totally devoted to him; he was the only man she had ever known intimately. Her husband, however, had been a diabetic with kidney problems who was on dialysis, had hypertension, and heart disease.

On the night Mrs. C's husband died, he had gotten up to go to the bathroom on several occasions. The first three times, when he arose, Mrs. C. rose with him. She would call to him to make sure he was okay. Each time he said yes and returned to bed. However, on the fourth time, Mrs. C. did not awaken when her husband went to the bathroom, and the next morning she found him dead on the bathroom floor. From that time, she could not sleep at night. Being unable to eat and crying constantly, she felt very depressed, had no energy, and lacked motivation to do anything. Although Mrs. C was a small woman, from the time of her husband's death only six weeks prior, she had lost ten pounds. She was beginning to have suicidal ruminations, although she had no plan to kill herself. Mrs. C's grief was beyond normal due to her unremitting guilt and suicidal preoccupation. Unquestionably, she had plunged into a major depression.

One factor which truly made her depressed and caused her to move into a region where she was both depressed and in a dark night was the blame she placed upon herself regarding her husband's death. Although it was extremely irrational, she blamed herself for her husband dying.

On many occasions during the therapy sessions, she would exclaim loudly to this doctor, "It's all my fault that he died. If I had only gotten up that last time, he wouldn't have died." She could not forgive herself for this sin of omission. Logic could not prevail, even though this doctor pointed out she had gotten up three times before he finally had the fatal episode, she could not reward herself for those efforts. When it was pointed out that her husband had a number of illnesses, any one of which could have killed him, that also fell upon deaf ears. She was in a dark night of profound depression and nothing could bring her out.

I began an intense treatment regime with weekly psychotherapy sessions and also antidepressant medications. Although it was effective in allaying some symptoms, such as insomnia, Mrs. C. remained quite depressed. Even telling her repeatedly that it was not her fault had little impact. She continued to bemoan her husband's death, blaming herself and saying that her failings were the reason he died.

Several antidepressant medications were tried, as well as regular psychotherapy. However, Mrs. C's depression persisted. Her family and church members also told her that losing her husband was destined to happen, and that she had no reason to feel guilty. Finally, it began to sink into her mind. Mrs. C made several moves which transported her through depression and despair and moved her through the dark night of the soul.

One of the first changes occurred as she began to accept that her husband was indeed gone, and there was nothing she could have done to prevent it. The minister at her church encouraged Mrs. C to go back to work. His suggestion was very important because she was so depressed that, although she had worked diligently for almost thirty years, following her husband's death she was unable to work at all. She had difficulty eating, sleeping, or doing anything. I had to place Mrs. C on disability and she was on it for nine months.

In order to go back to work, Mrs. C had to resolve a number of her depressive symptoms if not all of them. As she began to forgive herself of any error she might have made and realized she had done all that was humanly possible, the symptoms began to subside. I am not sure if she ever stopped blaming herself for what happened with her husband, but I am sure that she began to forgive herself for what happened. With encouragement from her minister, her family, and me, she was able to go back to work. Following releasing Mrs. C to go back to work, I never saw her again.

Mrs. C is a strong example of the power of grief to push one into a profound depression and enter into a night of despair and soul-searching. She also illustrates the power of acceptance and forgiveness to overcome, not only a clinically significant major depression, but also a spiritual crisis. She felt she had committed a sin worthy of punishment and even death. She had actually considered suicide. However, as she progressed and accepted her deficits as a human being, she began to change. As she moved to the point of self-forgiveness, she developed a greater capacity for self-love.

During Mrs. C's treatment, she was referred to a grief support group. There she learned that she was not the only one who had significant losses. She was not separate from others or singled out by the universe. As she reconnected with others and her church, she began to change. Once she terminated therapy, she still had quite a way to go before full recovery, but she was evolving and growing.

Another factor that can lead to severe depression and dwelling in the bleakness of the shadow is the change which occurs in the various stages of life. As we move from infancy into old age, our psyche goes through numerous transitions. We overcome many blockages along our path towards development and maturity. One of the tasks of young adulthood is forging one's own identity. If one is unable to perform that simple task, the consequences are great. It can be a catastrophe for a young person to be completely without direction. It can lead to a wasted and useless life. The thought that life might be in vain leads to an existential angst, which is unbearable.

I recall that as a young man of 24, I was in perfect health and had a girlfriend who loved me. I had a job, friends, and a family who cared about me as well. I was in graduate school, taking courses, but I did not know why I was taking them. Despite all of the things that looked good on the surface, I was significantly depressed. Although I was in the sunshine of my life, my spirit was in darkness. I did not know what I was on this earth to do. I did not have a clue.

My girlfriend, who loved me, grew tired of seeing me moping around so depressed. She referred me to a psychotherapist who had an office on the college campus. Tired of being in despair, I went. It was one of the most significant moves of my life. Through counseling, testing and reflection, I finally found my course, my purpose, which eventually led me into psychiatry and ultimately the ministry. In many ways my life was saved. I can bear testimony to a statement by Carl Jung, the famed psychiatrist, who said, "I observed that a directed life is in general better, richer, and healthier than an aimless one."[3]

Parents often define themselves in terms of their children. When their children are young demanding their attention and needing their help, they often feel and believe they are doing something with their lives. Once the children are grown and leave home, some are suddenly at a loss. They find that they don't have anything in their lives that is important to do. There is a void, often called the "empty nest syndrome." Rather than looking at it as an opportunity to find another direction in life, some mourn the loss of the children, no matter how fine a job they may have done. They dwell on memories of the past and wander into a valley of memories from which they cannot escape.

To overcome the painful feelings associated with looking into the void that one now has, one needs to begin thinking of taking care of oneself. All the years have been devoted to the children. Now the time can be devoted to oneself and to one's own personal growth and evolvement. Now is the time for spiritual exploration, as well as lavishing attention, which was spent on the children, upon oneself.

Often, as the person becomes accustomed to the new way of life, as he becomes more able to take care of himself and becomes interested in the spiritual ideals and philosophies which can help him grow into a higher consciousness, something happens. The children come back. Often they come back with grandchildren. For those who never got beyond the empty nest syndrome, they are delighted. They can go back into the past through doing the same activities they had done for 20 or 30 years. Although in the world they are delighted, spiritually they may be stunted. They will repeat the past and may not grow or enter into the time of purgation. They are afraid of the dark.

The ones who have found value in the new phase of life often begin to pursue inner illumination and may enter into the dark and their time of purgation. If so, they find themselves torn. Having embarked on a journey through the darkness towards the light, they want to continue. A different type of depression may approach them. The depression is a regret, a disappointment with having to abandon the journey temporarily. It is a journey, which they dreaded before, but now they have begun to anticipate. Their challenge is to throw upon their children the love they do feel for them and to assist them as much as they can while somehow continuing their journey because they can never go back to the way they were before.

Retirement also can lead to a dysphoric mood and to a downcast feeling towards life. It happens when a person has invested his entire life in his work, the job is how the person defines himself. He says, "I am an engineer," or "I am a surgeon," or "I am an artist." Regardless of the description, it is how he views himself. It can be a janitor or a clerk. The job description does not matter. What is important is the identification the person has with it. Once he is bereft of the title, he is lost. He has no purpose for being. It is the reason some people have difficulty with retirement.

Again, rather than looking at retirement as an opportunity to explore new ventures and ideas, rather than looking at it as having time which one never had before to delve into mysteries, the person looks upon the time as a time of "nothing to do" and a time of boredom. It is because he is stuck in the past. It is far better to look towards where he is going. Retirement is a problem for him, but there is no problem within consciousness. Consciousness perceives the problem and looks for solutions. As we delve into our intellect and allow our intuition to lead us, we find new ideas and new ways of living. Retirement is a time when we can truly dedicate ourselves to God and to helping others. We have the time, time we never had before. However, we have to look at the mysteries. We have to be able to see into the boredom and the uncertainty. If we are able to look into the abyss of anxiety concerning our lives and ourselves, we can use the intellect given us by the divine mind, which dwells in us all, to meet the challenge and resolve the situation. As we do so, we move forward along our spiritual journey and we move towards the light.

The retirees had made a profound error. They identified themselves with an earthly occupation rather than with that which they truly are. Once their intuition stirs them to think of their true nature, they can divest themselves of the earthy garments of employment and put on the clothes of purification.

Another precipitant, which can plunge a person into darkness and despair, is a personal crisis of extreme stress. It is often a turning point for better or for worse. When the trauma strikes, one is taken out of his usual state of well being. If he is a healthy individual or even in a state of comfort in which he functions marginally and has some problems, he is transformed into a state of pain. A person will utilize all of his resources to get out of the painful state and go back to a point of equilibrium and homeostasis. However, he often does not succeed. Many times he finds himself repeating painful patterns. He becomes entrenched in the very deficits, which are causing him to have the problems he is experiencing. As his efforts fail and his self-esteem deteriorates, he becomes quite distraught. Spiritually his eyes are closed and he does not see himself as the son of the living God, but often as a demon in the flesh. It is then that he is truly in a deep dungeon and he has to expel disparaging forces in order to return to a state of wholeness.

A severe accident whereby one is injured to the point of death and disability could easily be a personal crisis and lead to self-examination and tenuous physical rehabilitation. There are many other events and/or triggers which can cause an emotional crisis and lead to deep depression or a spiritual emergency.

Almost anything can lead to a crisis, depending on one's perspective and point of view. A hazardous situation will cause some people to become panicked, but will only inspire some others to gird their loins. It is no accident that the Chinese characters for crisis are the same ones used for opportunity. In the truest sense, no matter how the person responds, the crisis is still a golden opportunity, although it may not feel that way to the person who is undergoing it. The word crisis implies change. Something is being transformed, whether for good or for ill.

Common factors, which lead to emotional crises, are financial losses or pressures. If one finds himself in a large amount of debt, it can definitely lead to an emotional crisis because one often wonders whether he will be able to support himself, whether he will be able to eat and keep a roof over his head and the head of his family. To have to dwell on such things can definitely lead to emotional crises. However, if one has the perspective that everything is going to be all right, and he is equal to the task, it will not upset him as much as someone who sees himself as hopeless and not able to overcome the large amount of money he owes. No matter how he looks at it, the individual will also have to examine himself and look within for that is where the spiritual work begins.

Job pressure or the actual loss of a job is also a significant precipitant. Inner personal conflict with a loved one also is a common cause of crisis and emotional conflict. It is particularly hard if it is something leading to a divorce or separation. However, it can be something as simple as a new baby entering the family and the adjustments one will have to make for him or her entering the family unit. All can lead to crises, and what is important is how one chooses to respond.

Self-examination and turning within is necessary if there will be true growth. One's beliefs and the values which are important in life are examined. Hopefully there is transformation and growth, but often there is deterioration and neuroses that enter instead. Entering the night is a must. Moving through the darkness, either with a guide or with one's own inner guide, has to be done. Only then can one return to wholeness. Only then can one purge himself of undesirable attitudes, beliefs, and characteristics and so move himself into higher consciousness. As psychiatrist Dr. Peter Sifneos states in his book *Short Term Psychotherapy and Emotional Crises*, "Only after an individual has been able to overcome the turbulent disruption of his emotional crises is he able to return to a mentally healthy level of functioning."[4]

NOTE

1. St John of the Cross, *Dark Night of the Soul*, Image Books, New York, NY, 1990, pp 33-34.
2. Ibid, page 37
3. Carl Jung, *Modern Man in Search of a Soul*, HBJ Books, New York, NY and London, England, 1933, page 112.
4. Peter Sifneos, MD, *Short Term Psychotherapy and Emotional Crisis*, Harvard University Press, Cambridge, Massachusetts, 1972, page 29.

Chapter 2

PURGATION OR DEPRESSION

The significance of depression and how it differs from the Dark Night of the Soul.

Most of us can tell when we are depressed. We feel it in our bones. There is an aching in our hearts, in our very being, maybe an agony. Every day seems cloudy, and it seems as if the sun refuses to shine. At our worst, we are beyond even thoughts of suicide. We are simply apathetic and cannot move. We are literally petrified with depression. The question then is when is a state of dysfunction and despair more than simply depression? When is it truly the dark night of the soul? What is the difference?

The mystic Saint John of the Cross tells us it can be difficult to make a distinction. In fact, someone can be both severely depressed and also enduring the dark night of the soul. It appears that depression and the spiritual journey through darkness are intricately linked. However, the fact that someone is undergoing a strong depression does not mean that he is taking steps along the path of spiritual purgation. Saint John of the Cross tells us there are several things by which we can know that we are truly moving towards the light.

The human soul has a sensual sense and a spiritual sense. As we undergo the pain of releasing our imperfections and grieving our mental errors, we reach a point where we derive little or no pleasure from physical things. The joys of the world, which once delighted us have very little or no meaning. Our disposition changes and it is difficult to experience pleasure, and there is a lack of interest in almost everything. When the inability to experience pleasure is global, it is certain that one is in the midst of a strong depression. It is also very probable that the same person is experiencing the dark night of the soul. The key difference is that the person who is going through the soul-searching is concerned about his care and grief from not serving God. He or she flogs himself for not being a good and faithful servant of the Lord. If someone is simply depressed, there is no such concern. He is simply lost in his own gloom and wonders if he will ever see the light of day. Neither person, when he is in his deepest hole, expects to ever see dawn break into his life again, but both will. The difference is, one will grow spiritually and the other will not.

Even in the midst of his time of trial, the person who is traversing the path of consciousness is doing spiritual seeking. He tries to meditate, but finds no comfort in it. The one who is depressed asks God why God has not answered his prayers. The one on the path asks God instead for forgiveness for his wrong doings and to help him find how to serve. It is a small but significant difference. Both may feel a need to be punished. There will be thoughts of worthlessness and being "no good." Most will lose sight of their Divine nature and forget that they are always priceless and worthy in the sight of the Divine. The spiritual seeker cannot find comfort in his former spiritual practices because he has been pushed to a new level. The old ways do not serve the new being who is emerging. A deeper practice and a deeper means of service have to be found. As the spiritual seeker pushes through the sense purgation of his soul, he begins to experience the stirring for a closer union with God. He begins to put forth mighty efforts to bring about the union. Of course, the efforts fail and he is made to realize that mental and physical means cannot bring about a closer connection with Spirit. Spirit alone can do it. Nonetheless, the frustration and the strong yearning can bring about another depressive episode. It can even seem worse than the initial one. What is good, in a sense, is that most people do not get to the second depressive episode which is associated with purgation of the spiritual part of the soul. The ones who do are the ones who have truly devoted themselves totally to spiritual evolution. They are the contemplatives. They are contemplatives because they have worked hard to raise their consciousness and have reached the point where the physical or mental effort cannot further them along their journey.

Now is the time to be still. Now is the time to turn within. For those who are fortunate enough to reach this phase of their passage through the shadow, there is a strong yearning for God's love. There is an urge to feel the peace of God and a desire to merge with the Holy Spirit in a divine union. The person who is fighting a clinical depression may have an indisposition of the body and require anti-depressant medications to overcome his afflictions. He or she may require psychotherapy, group therapy, and other forms of treatment. The person who is experiencing the journey through darkness may also require those same things. As their symptoms alleviate, the person suffering only from clinical depression will return to his previous life. Sometimes he may do better than he did before the depression. He will begin to experience joy in the things he once did before. The person who is spiritually seeking will still have a need to persevere. Although the clinical depression has alleviated, there is still something missing. Often the sense of something missing will cause another depression or will prolong the depression which is being treated. As has been said, now it is time to surrender. Now is the time to let go and let God.

Joel Goldsmith instructs us in what we are to do now, which is "To close ourselves in tight and realize that we need not resist evil. The battle is not ours, but God's."[1] We are further instructed to trust the Holy Spirit and allow it to do its work with us by the instruction we are given from scripture. "Not by might, nor by power, but by my spirit, sayeth the Lord."[2]

Although it appears that every dark night of the soul is associated with depression, it does not seem that every depression is associated with the dark night of the soul. Many depressions have no apparent spiritual significance. Of course, a person can give spiritual significance to practically anything, but he or she would simply be deluding himself or herself. There is a reason for everything, but sometimes a depression is simply a depression.

I believe it is important to be able to distinguish a clinical depression from a spiritual ordeal. With the vital elements of a journey through the shadow having been highlighted, it is now necessary to concentrate on the symptoms of the depressive disorders.

Depression is universal. Everyone has been depressed at one time or another in his life. Who hasn't risen on the wrong side of the bed, or had a bad day? Usually, the moments are fleeting and very short-lived, and the next day we return to our optimistic and cheerful moods. The depression is no more than a cloud which briefly swept past the face of the sun. It is quickly forgotten. However, there are more lingering depressions which can affect our lives. When they are mild and do not impact upon us very strongly, we may call them the "blahs" or being "down in the dumps." When the feelings persist and we have more bad days than good days, then that is when problems begin.

Finally, there is a condition which in American culture we call "the blues." It is colorfully described in many songs. Although the lyrics are often playful, the condition is serious and can even be fatal. Two lines from the renowned blues song "Trouble in Mind" describe the condition. "Trouble in mind, I'm blue, but I won't be blue always. The sun's going to shine in my back door, some day." If the person who has the blues believes that there is going to be a break and the light will shine in his or her life; that is a good sign. However, if he does not believe it, matters become significantly worse, as is described in the second line of the song, "I'm going to lay my head on that lonesome railroad line and let the 2:19 train ease my troubled mind." Here, the person is saying, "I've given up; I'm going to end my life." When depression is severe, people entertain thoughts of suicide and even make plans and complete them.

I have alluded to several types of depressions. Indeed, in psychiatric literature, there are a number of classifications and subclassifications. In order to keep the types simple, it is best to describe what is called a major depression disorder or a major depressive episode. It is when depression becomes clinically significant and quite severe. It is the dejected mood and condition which one has to overcome before a person can even enter into the spiritual trial they are destined to undertake. At the point of major depression, one is simply concerned with returning to some degree of earthly well being.

St. John of the Cross describes the condition as a physical indisposition. The person who suffers from a severe depression, which is often incapacitating him and keeping him from working or enjoying social relationships, is suffering from the "humours of the body." The humours is a medieval way of saying that something is wrong with the biochemistry of the person's being. The individual will need aggressive treatment and care. In medieval times, they may have been given herbs, brew, blood-letting and things of that sort. Nowadays, they are given antidepressants and aggressive psychotherapy. Also, sometimes the person is involved in group therapy and various health-promoting activities. The most severe depressions may require electroconvulsive therapy or shock treatment. Despite the stigma electroconvulsive therapy has been given, it has been found to be very effective for the most refractory cases of depression.

What are the major criteria of a major depression? What is it that clinicians look for and people should be aware of in order to recognize a major depression? It is important because, if one can recognize it, it can be treated and corrected. It is one of the most treatable conditions there is in psychology. The most prominent feature is a pervasive depressed mood which a person has most of the day nearly every day. It is unrelenting. The mood must persist for at least two weeks before one can begin to entertain a diagnosis of major depression; but, moods have been known to endure for much longer than two weeks, even into years. When the person is very depressed, there is a diminished interest in nearly all of the things that he or she was previously involved in doing. There is a significant loss of pleasure in the activities in which he was able to find joy before. Many times the person loses his appetite and does not enjoy eating and will sometimes have a significant weight loss. Sleeping is disturbed so that he finds himself waking up in the middle of the night unable to return to sleep; or, if he does not wake up in the middle of the night, he wakes up early in the morning, two or three hours earlier than he usually awakens and cannot return to sleep. When he does rise, he is tired and does not feel rested. Other people make comments to him that he looks like he has slowed down, or if not that, that he is very restless. The normal activity level is disturbed. Even though sleep loss causes him to have some tiredness, the level of fatigue and low energy that he experiences cannot be accounted for by simply not having enough sleep. The person is very fatigued and very tired. There is also a feeling of worthlessness as though he does not deserve anything and there is a decided lack of self-esteem. Again, I refer to one of the blues songs popularized by the great blues artist BB King. A line from one of his songs says, "Don't nobody love me but my mama, and she could be jiving too." In this song, he is suspicious of anybody who looks upon him as a worthwhile human being because that is not the way he sees himself.

Other symptoms consist of a decided inability to concentrate or focus. Finally, there are recurrent thoughts of death. The person may not actually be thinking of committing suicide, but there are thoughts along the theme of, "I wish I was dead." There are also often crying spells. A person will find himself crying for no apparent reason several times a week. When a depressed mood combined with four or more of the symptoms previously described are present, the person reaches the criteria for a major depression. When that happens and he is suffering in his job and/or his social relationships, he needs to seek immediate psychiatric treatment. If he is suicidal, he will need to be hospitalized. It is the phase where we are dealing with the humours and the physical indisposition. It is necessary to deal with the condition clinically before attempting to set foot on the path through the shadows.

Fortunately, in the twenty-first century, the condition is easily treated. There are literally dozens of antidepressants from which to choose and use according to a patient's particular makeup. Also, there are effective psychotherapies, such as Cognitive Behavioral Therapy, which can be used to help treat the person along with the medications, or sometimes in and of themselves, although, in most instances, the condition will not improve without the use of medicines. A combination of therapy and medication together gives the best outcome.

Even without treatment, forty percent of people will resolve from the condition in approximately six month's time or longer. Another twenty percent will also resolve from the condition but will have symptoms that linger and be somewhat debilitating. Perhaps forty percent will return to their previous level of functioning. The problem is that six months of severe depression is a long time. It is long enough to lose one's job and also be divorced. It is best that the person receive the treatment he needs so he can return to a good level of functioning as soon as possible.

There is another type of depression which is more characterologic. Currently, it bears the diagnosis of dysthymic disorder and was previously called a chronic depressive neurosis. The condition is not as severe as major depression and, acutely, is not as disabling. However, by its very definition, it must be present at least two years before it can be diagnosed. So, what is described is two years of misery. A dysthymic disorder can be present in children as well as adults. If it is present in the perpetually unhappy child or adolescent, the condition is diagnosed if it lasts persistently for a year or longer. It does not have to last the two years which is the required threshold for adults. During the time, the person has a depressed mood for most of the day, for more days than not.

Two or more of the following symptoms also need to be present: 1) poor appetite or overeating, 2) insomnia or hypersomnia, 3) poor energy or fatigue, 4) low self-esteem, 5) poor concentration or difficulty in making decisions, and 6) feelings of hopelessness. It is noted that the number of symptoms required to make the diagnosis are not as many as are necessary to make the diagnosis of clinical major depression. Dysthymic disorder is not as severe. However, it is still damaging, and one is not in his true state of enjoyment. Also, because it is lasting, it impacts on a person's ability to work and have good relationships.

If one is made aware that he or she suffers from dysthymic disorder, it is best to enter into a type of psychotherapy and not to think of himself as suffering for spiritual reasons. A person has simply acquired bad habits and has become entrenched in an attitude of unhappiness which can last his entire life if he is not careful. Insightful counseling, affirmations, and support groups which validate a person's right to well being can help someone through dysthymic disorder and enable him to get to the point where he can actually embark on the journey through the dark night of the soul.

The final type of depression that I will touch upon is known as an adjustment disorder with depressive features. In the old literature, it was formerly categorized as a reactive depression. It is what happens when an individual reacts excessively emotionally to a stressor. Here, he is so impacted by what happened that he is now so depressed that he has difficulty with his job or functioning socially. His depressive mood usually begins within three months following the stressing event and usually will clear up within six months. However, what the person does during the time to address the stressor will determine how healthy he will be at the end of the six months. Crisis intervention and a means of addressing the stressor are important in returning to good health. It is necessary to help the person look at what has happened not as a catastrophe, but as a challenge and an opportunity to grow.

Many different events can be the stressor. It can be a painful divorce or the joyful birth of a child. Both require dramatic change. The loss of a beloved spouse is perhaps the greatest stressor of all. All of them can be overcome. How one deals with the stressor will determine his future hopes and ability to continue along life's journey into illumination.

As has been said, depression is a ubiquitous human experience. Everyone feels its pangs at some time in their life. The degree of the condition can vary considerably. It can go from a very mild, brief transient state to one that is severe, chronic, and disabling which may last for years. Although depression is quite common, it is still not normal. Like anxiety, another emotional state, there is a reason for depression's existence.

The well-known emotion of anxiety was a key to the survival of the species, Homo Sapiens. Whenever danger threatened, our nervous system would go into a state of hyper arousal. It would move us into action whenever the tiger was stalking us as prehistoric man, or when our lives are in danger now as modern man. Anxiety warns us of impending danger from some external force and mobilizes our bodies to a state of fight or flight.

Depression, too, has a much needed function. A depressed condition is a signal that something is vitally wrong. It does not announce that we are in some immediate danger. Instead, it whispers to us that something is amiss. A vital ingredient of our being is no longer there. Whatever is missing could be from any part of our psychosocial system. It can even be spiritual. Dr. Aaron Beck. the originator of Cognitive Therapy, states "It is relatively easy to detect the dominant theme in the statement of the moderately or severely depressed patient. He regards himself as lacking some element or attribute that he considers essential for his happiness."[3]

The loss of that which is desired can often be traced to a "precipitating event." It is often a discrete, traumatic occurrence where the object that we desire and value is lost to us. It, in fact, may not be lost, but what is important is that we perceive that it is gone. In the time of depression, we have to determine what is being released and what has to be changed.

There are numerous types of precipitating events that can plunge a person into a depressive state. Biologically, it can be as simple as an elite athlete who is no longer able to perform up to his previous expectations. As he ages, he loses a step or some degree of skill. Although it is expected, it can still lead to a depression. The athlete is now forced to sit down and examine what he is going to do for the rest of his life; what other changes he is going to have to make. More dramatically, it can be a severe, life-threatening illness, such as metastatic cancer or a disabling stroke. A previously high functioning person may be disabled to the point of death and total dependency on others. He then grieves the loss of his physical abilities and his total dependence on others. The contributing factor as to what is amiss is very obvious. Depression will endure so long as the person cannot release his or her thoughts concerning the condition and make peace with the new body. Optimism and acceptance are changes which can alter the entire character of the depression and in some cases lead to healing, not only emotionally, but also biologically.

Perhaps the greatest precipitating factor that leads to depression is in the psychosocial arena. It has been statistically documented and proven that nothing is as devastating as the loss of a highly treasured and beloved spouse. It is not uncommon for people who have lived together in a loving marriage for 40, 50 or more years to die within months or even weeks of one another.

I had the unpleasant experience of watching the mother of a dear friend of mine literally grieve herself to death following the death of her husband of many years. It was her second marriage and they had a conflicted, but nevertheless close, relationship. They raised three children together and the eldest child was in his 40s at the time of the husband's death. She lived about a year after his passing and was never the same. Many of us have borne witness to similar stories which have had the same type of ending. Even people who do not have as long a time together and have marriages which end unhappily can experience a severe loss which leads to a lasting depression. Often, one of the divorced partners goes into a depressive state which may even lead to a violent or suicidal act.

Yet, we also hear of other tales of people who have lost a beloved life partner and still manage to function just fine after the person is gone. They grieve, they cry, they go through all of the rituals of releasing the beloved to the other side. Then, they manage to move on with their lives. They may even have lost their spouse in their 70s or even in their 80s. Somehow, they recover. We wonder what the difference is. What is the secret of the survivors? We begin by looking at the meaning of the depression and finding out what is amiss.

The central them in all depression is loss. When a key psychosocial relationship is disrupted, the one who is experiencing the loss may have the perception that an intricate part of his or herself is gone. It is more than the passing of the beloved and the changes which will have to take place. The person sees it as if a part of him has been taken. More than that, he looks at it as if nothing can replace what has been taken and he will be forever less than whole.

The ones who survive well are the ones who accept that something which is irreplaceable has been taken. However, they are left with precious memories and know that nothing can ever make them less than whole or less than what they truly are. They may look upon it as if they are a fully orbed spiritual being no matter what happens to them in their life, or they may decide psychologically they have enough to continue to have a meaningful life experience.

It helps tremendously if there is a strong support system. Often, there are children who can support the person through the loss. Also, people who have lost loved ones with whom they had been for many years can see their loved one in the children who remain. Ministers, spiritual practitioners, church members, and prayer partners who support the bereaved and see them as children of the living God going through a meaningful experience are very important in helping them overcome their ordeal.

What is amiss is the perception of being less than whole. There has been, in fact, a real loss which cannot be denied. The problem begins when one thinks that nothing can suffice to help replace the loss. A person makes it a problem if he thinks he needs something which would be just like what has been lost. What has been lost is unique and cannot be replaced. Something else, however, can occur which, in turn, can bring comfort, satisfaction and meaning to life. Spiritually and psychologically, the depression is a signal to find something that is meaningful in order to continue with life. It is a signal to accept what has been lost--cherish it and honor it in memory. The person must look for how to give what has been lost its own significance while, at the same time, releasing it. Coretta Scott King made her life more meaningful by continuing the work of her assassinated husband, Reverend Doctor Martin Luther King, Jr. She made sure that the Center for Nonviolence in Atlanta continued, and she traveled the United States and the world, continuing to spread his message of peace.

It is important to retain the knowledge that one is whole, perfect and complete no matter what losses he has experienced. As one regains the knowledge of his or her sovereign self, despite the loss, the person moves through depression and moves through the dark nights of the soul. Also, an essential thing is to have patience. The healing process is taking place, no matter what it might look like on the surface. It takes at least a year, during which time one undergoes anniversaries and also special occasions, such as birthdays and graduations, before one truly begins to overcome the significant loss of a loved one. After the year is over, life gradually improves until one day one may look back, think of memories of the beloved, and although tears may occasionally be shed, actually smile.

On other occasions, the precipitating factor which causes a depression is unclear. It can be an insidious mental event. There can be abuse during childhood or in one's relationships which erodes one's self-esteem. Biologically, one can be predisposed to depression by having a very strong family history with a number of individuals in the family tree who have been treated for depressive illnesses. Whether through an unfriendly environment, dysfunctional relationships, or through biological predisposition, mentally we can find ourselves in what is called a "funk." When it is unclear why, it is time to look inside. The depression is a signal to pause and reflect. There may not be a readily identifiable external precipitating factor, but there is an ongoing condition brought on by them. We have allowed that which is without to effect that which is within and to alter our state of well being.

Cases of environmental factors which have been ongoing can lead to poor self-esteem and a distorted self image. If we are biologically predisposed to depression physiologically, we may be going into a depressive episode and may need antidepressant medications to bring us out of it. Here, it is important to recognize the sense of loss of self. A person in a depressive state of this type blames everything on himself. No matter what someone else may have done, he may decide that it is really his fault. No matter how spotless his behavior towards others, he may decide that he is a terrible being who deserves to be punished for whatever thing he has done in life.

On one such occasion, I had the opportunity to counsel and treat an older Jewish woman who had been active during the Civil Rights movement. She was in her late 60s when I met her and she had one child, an adult son in his forties. As we struggled to help her overcome her depression, she wailed in one session about how she was unlovable. She made every attempt to convince me of how horrible she was. Finally, as she continued to sing the song of "nobody loves me," and "I am unlovable," I stopped arguing with her. We took a pause in the session. After a brief silence, I said to her, "I bet your son loves you." She thought about it, and then, we both broke out into a hearty laugh. We laughed so hard that tears came to our eyes. Then I said to her, "Now that we've disproved that theory, we can go on." She never again said that she was unlovable, at least not to me.

The woman's case illustrates the fact that mentally we have to look at what is amiss, what the depression is telling us, and realize that we are unique individuals who are worthy of love. Our creator accepts us all on this planet and it is best we accept ourselves. The assumption that we are worthless and that people abuse us because we are so bad is a distorted belief. We are never worthless and those who abuse us did so for their own reasons. It was never our fault and never will be. What is important is that we decide we are of value and do not deserve to be abused and move on into a more healthy and wholesome climate. As we mentally reorder our thinking and lose the distortions of worthlessness, victimhood, and being the person who causes everybody else's problems, we move into health. We accept responsibility for our lives and allow others to accept responsibility for what they do. We do not blame what they did on ourselves. Mentally, we allow ourselves to be free. We allow ourselves to make mistakes and to be forgiven for them, and also, we allow ourselves to be loved for who and what we are. Psychologically and spiritually, the truth is that we are deserving. Both spiritual and psychological literature supports the fact.

Finally, there is the type of depression where there is no identifiable external precipitating factor. Here, we encounter the spiritual angst, which is part and parcel of the dark night of the soul. We may have reached a point in life when things have lost their meaning to us. Our psychological development may have reached a dead end. Our spiritual practices, meditations, and reflections may no longer bring satisfaction. We don't know what to do next. We are without direction. We are lost. Regardless of age or circumstance, there are few things as depressing as a life without meaning. When it happens, the person is in a true crisis. The loss of all meaning and purpose in life is what is happening. It is what the depression is telling the person who is experiencing it. The task then is to be put on the path of spiritual evolution and enter into the dark night of the soul.

Even if it is with fear and trepidation, it is better to confront the crisis and deal with what is transpiring in one's life than to try to avoid the pain by running away from the issues. Only by entering into the shadow and moving through it can one find satisfaction and a new meaning to life. Psychologically, it is a time of assessing one's values. It is a time to look at where one wants to be in ten years or at the end of life. What does one want to accomplish in this life and leave as a legacy? Things of that sort help give meaning to life psychologically.

Spiritually, one begins to look at one's current spiritual views and asks "Why isn't this satisfying to me now?" It is time to move from spiritual adolescence into spiritual adulthood. It is no longer sufficient to play with meditation, or be a dilettante and jump from one spiritual practice to another. There is no satisfaction in being into crystals one day and into chanting the next. It is necessary to look deep within and consider one's personal relationship with God. What comes in from the center of one's soul determines what the new direction is to be. The process can be painful, even excruciating, but it is necessary.

Fortunately, there are people who have gone before who can help lead the way and shine light onto the path that has to be trodden. We replace the loss of meaning in life and the loss of satisfaction with a new relationship with the Divine and a renewed sense of purpose after having accessed our deepest personal values. We more than make up for the losses spiritually and psychologically which we have experienced and move into a higher vibration of life as we gain new knowledge and experience.

One of the most important things about depression is, not only does it show us that something is amiss, but it also informs us that there are lessons which need to be learned. A very popular definition of insanity is "doing the same things over and over while expecting a different result." If one performs a certain action, it will produce the same result it produced before unless there has been a change somewhere. If one mixes yellow with blue, he will always make the color green. It would be illogical to mix the two colors and expect to create the color red. Nowhere is the repetition of destructive habits which produce the same undesirable results more prevalent than in depression.

People engage in the same repetitive behaviors over and over and expect to feel better. They expect their lives to change without changing themselves or making any fundamental changes in their behavior. It is impossible. The ongoing pains of depression inform us that we have to change what we are doing. Not only is it important to alter the way we are thinking, we also have to alter our behaviors. It is important to explore and obtain new habits and a new way of being in the world. Even if someone is not certain of what he is supposed to do, it is important to try something different.

The depressed person is afraid to make mistakes. The big mistake is not making an effort to do something different. Even if it does not work, the person learns from the experience. In this moment, I want all persons who may suffer from depression to know that it is okay to make mistakes. The only real mistake is to persist in error.

So then, the depressed person begins to seek counsel. He learns from people who have had a similar experience to the one he has and then discovered alternative ways of doing something. He may engage in brain storming, either alone or with others.

The solutions which are discovered are tested. They are put into practice into the life of the person who is seeking new ways of being and acting. If they work, the person keeps them and improves upon them. If they do not work, they are discarded and the person continues to embark upon finding a new way of being. Lessons are learned, unlearned and re-learned until the depression lifts. When the mood becomes elevated and the activities which the person is engaging in are bringing harmony and well being into his life, the lesson has been learned.

As unlikely as it may seem, the person may benefit from going through a depression. I cannot think of anyone who would want to experience the pain involved, but if he or she can endure it, the outcome can be great. Even beyond that, if a spiritual seeker can reach into his angst and confront his dark side, he will emerge more whole and spiritually integrated than ever before in his life. It cannot happen without first paying attention to whatever is amiss, becoming aware of it and making necessary key changes. If one persists in practicing old habits and ways of being, it is a fast highway to destruction.

Psychologists have discovered that a person who finds a solution to a problem and has success is more likely to have success with the next problem. The reason is that as he learns from his experience, he develops new ways of dealing with life; he has broadened his repertoire of behaviors, and expanded his knowledge. It is an upward spiral, and the person tends to improve and become healthier. It is also true that as one finds success in navigating through depression and through his spiritual trials, learning takes place. Insight and revelation happen. It is the task of the person going through the process to accept the teachings and revelations. He must endeavor to integrate them into his life. When he does, it is like Job after he endured the many trials and tribulations during his time of despair. When he surrendered to God and became humble before Him, he was rewarded with wealth far exceeding what he had before. In like manner, when we surrender to the process, accept the loss, embrace the new, and learn what we need to know to grow deeper into our awareness of God and of ourselves, the benefits and rewards are immeasurable. They happen at every level of our lives – personal, financial, health-wise and spiritually.

Although depression is part and parcel of the dark night of the soul, the reverse is not true. A person can be in the throes of depression and have no spiritual activity going on in his psyche whatsoever. He is simply depressed. He is in despair because his sweetheart left him, or because he lost a profitable and rewarding job. There are many causes that can lead a person into a state of depression. As was previously mentioned, one can distinguish between a depression, no matter how mild or severe, and the dark night of the soul. The feeling tones of pain and despair are present in both. However, there are a number of key differences.

There are several factors which are present when one is enduring the dark night of the soul that are absent in experiencing depression alone. A necessary, but not sufficient, condition of the dark night of the soul is the emotional state of anhedonia. It is a Greek term which means there is an inability to experience pleasure. The person can find no enjoyment in anything. It is important because in the dark night, a person is not able to find satisfaction in any of his previous worldly pleasures. None of the music that he likes or the people who he enjoys gives him pleasure. He is not interested in wine, women or song. Worse, he also is not able to find satisfaction in his previous spiritual practices. Although meditation might bring some kind of temporary respite, it does not bring enjoyment. Scriptural readings are simply a literary exercise. Although anhedonia is present in the severest forms of depression such as depression with melancholia, its presence in the dark night of the soul is important because previous spiritual practices which brought relief no longer do so. It is a signal showing that he or she has to go deeper. Spiritually, one has to change. Something within has to be released and also something has to be embraced. It is the purgation that is going on which is part of the dark night of the soul.

Another necessary factor which distinguishes the journey through the darkness from mere depression is a fervent desire to serve God. Someone who is in mere depression may be crying "Woe is me," and that alone. Someone who is in the dark night will be asking himself, "What can I do to be a better servant to the Almighty?" He is in despair because he does not see himself as serving God. Not only is he not finding any joy in any of his previous practices, he now faults himself for not serving God in a more complete manner. The desire to serve God is so strong that it actually causes pain if one thinks he or she is found wanting. The person thinks he is "backsliding." However, nothing could be further from the truth. He is simply moving into a time of purging old habits which have to be changed. If it was only depression, he would have ambivalence and a weak will, but he is firm in his wanting to serve the Divine no matter how far he thinks he may have fallen.

Another important sign is when a person, in finding no satisfaction in anything whether material or spiritual, then becomes quiet. He must necessarily turn within. It is more than the isolation and avoidance of people that is characteristic of depression; it is more like a personal retreat. As did the prophets of old and Jesus Christ himself, the person goes away by himself to find himself. He is metaphorically spending forty days in the desert. If he survives the time and passes through it, he gathers strength. Some never resolve from so severe a trial. Some never overcome so severe a depression. Even with clinical help, everyone does not do so although, potentially, all can.

Literally in quietness and stillness, one finds his strength. The person has to surrender until the still small voice within speaks. When one has surrendered and is moved into solitude, so as to let the spirit within work, he is in the dark night of the soul. It helps to have some knowledge that God has placed one on the hidden path. It is only by turning within to God that can one walk through it. The Christ Presence, the Buddha Nature, the Divine Presence within, by whatever name it is called is that which shines its light upon the path and gives a person the guidance to walk through the dark night of the soul.

Finally, a very key factor which allows a person to know that he is going through the night of purgation is that of contemplation. The seeker is no longer a spiritual dilettante. There can be no satisfaction or growth from trying new things and dabbling in them. There is only misery to be found in gazing at crystals one week and following the latest New Age thought or trend the next. It becomes clear to an individual that spirituality is not a fashion. It is not a trend. It is a profoundly serious way of life. It finally hits him that he has to be spiritually committed. One cannot be even like the rich young man in the New Testament who wanted to follow Jesus. He asked the Master, "What should I do to gain salvation?" Jesus told him, "Give up all of your belongings, give up all your possessions, and follow me."[2] The young man was downhearted. He could not do what Jesus advised. He cherished his possessions. He is like a spiritual dilettante who enjoys dabbling, but cannot be serious. I imagine he was profoundly depressed as he realized his shortcomings and turned away from Jesus.

Contemplation means going into a state of consciousness where one meditates only on God. A person seeks to find a greater awareness of his or her union with the Divine. He seeks to know his God nature and to experience the feeling that he and the Father of the Essence of all creation are One. He contemplates making the commitment of a life dedicated to God. It is a process. It is not done in an instant for the great majority of people, although there are some who are so evolved that is done unto them even as they think it. For most of us, however, it is a process. We entertain the thought of a life dedicated to God, and we think of it more and more until it is our sole contemplation. Part of going through the process is letting go of the things to which we are attached, as was the case with the rich young man in the Bible, and letting go of old habits and ways which served us once but can serve no longer. No matter how dismal the mood may seem, the contemplation of a deep spiritual commitment to divine ideals and values, and to the Divine itself makes of it a purgation. It makes of it a passage through the dark night of the soul into the light.

There is yet another difference between the two emotional conditions which is true of major depression alone. The feeling tone for both depression and the dark night of the soul are similar and can be felt in our very bones. Major depression, however, is primarily an indisposition of the body. It does not dwell on spiritual matters. Bodily processes are disturbed and physically we are weakened. We are lukewarm in our will and our desire. We do not desire to serve God. We do not desire to serve anything. We are simply aware of our body and our psychic pain. The depression is in our blood, so to speak. It is what St. John calls, "The humours." He intuited, even back as long ago as the 16ᵗʰ century when he lived, that there was some kind of toxic fluid which was present in our body and was part of the depression. In fact, he thought it might be what caused the depression. Centuries later, psychiatrists, psychologists, and researchers have found that biochemicals in the body are altered in a state of lasting severe depression. The activating neurotransmitters, such as norepinephrine and serotonin are present in diminished levels in our blood. It is one of the reasons that antidepressant medication works. The medicines work to replenish or potentiate the actions of the activating neurotransmitters which are in our bloodstream. Preoccupation with the bodily processes to the exclusion of almost all else usually means one is not dealing with emerging from shadow, but is simply dealing with depression. With all due respect to the person who is suffering, truth be said, dealing with the depression alone is more than enough.

Another vital component of the dark night of the soul concerns love, specifically divine love. We all want love, no matter what our condition may be, so that is no distinguishing characteristic for anything. In both conditions, the person may not think himself worthy of love of any kind. So, that is not a distinguishing characteristic either. What makes for a distinct difference is something which is almost unperceivable initially. In fact, it may be unperceivable and happening only at an unconscious level. The spiritual seeker is passionately involved in wanting to serve God and move into contemplation so as to touch the divine presence within so that the divine presence acts toward him. Even in the midst of one's pain and sorrow, there is a movement which is taking place. The light of higher consciousness is being shone upon the person's innermost secrets and desires. Even on an unconscious level, they are being exposed and stripped away at the core. As the person adopts an attitude of surrendering to Spirit, Spirit begins to show its love for him and a divine fire within begins to burn away his habits and addictions which have bound the person and kept him from moving forward along his spiritual path. St. John of the Cross refers to it as, "an enkindling of love."

The divine light of the Holy Spirit shines upon a person's soul and burns away sensual desires and imperfections. The soul is stripped and left bare. What remains must resonate with love for the infusion of divine love is what has cleansed the soul and elevated the spiritual consciousness of the recipient. It is the point in the dark night of purification where the seeker passionately desires to be immersed in the Divine and actually begins to understand the first great commandment, "And thou shalt love the Lord thy God with all of thine heart, with all thine soul, and with all thine might."[4] When one considers it, the great commandment is common to all religions and spiritual traditions. It is not simply the law of love for Christians but of Muslims, Jews, and anyone who seeks a relationship with God. There is no conflict. As a result, everyone, no matter what his spiritual orientation, is subject to the dark night of the soul and to the enkindling of divine love which accompanies it. The journey is a process of purgation. Without the infusion and enkindling of divine love, it is impossible to make it.

A very important distinction between a simple depression, no matter how severe, and one which involves the dark night of the soul is how one views himself when he is in his emotional state. To the seeker, there is an inner knowing that the misery that has been placed upon him is not a random thing. Even though at times the person may feel it is all for nothing, ultimately he seeks an inner meaning behind it all. At some level, the soul knows that God Himself has brought it to the purgation of the dark night through which it is traveling. If the spiritual seeker does not believe that he or she has been chosen to suffer, at least at some intuitive level, there is still a conviction that darkness has been brought to his spirit so that the time of dwelling in the shadow may give it light. Yes, the night humbles him and makes him miserable, but he will be exalted and raised to a higher level of consciousness and spiritual understanding.

The person who is involved only in depression does not see any hope or meaning in the tribulation through which he is going. He sees himself as a victim who has suffered a great loss. The loss can be real or imagined, but he believes he deserves to have what was taken from him taken and, worse, he believes there is nothing he can do about it. The person laments that life is meaningless. There is a random senseless quality to his suffering and illogical self-depreciating conclusions only make it worse.

As previously mentioned, the primary factor which seems to be characteristic of all depressions is a sense of loss. In a typical depression, an object can usually be identified which has been taken from the individual. It can be something which is material, or it can be in the form of a relationship. There are a number of stressors which experts agree will usually precipitate a depression in most individuals. Numerous clinicians and researchers agree on the precipitating events which will now be mentioned as being a harbinger of depression in the great majority of individuals.

1.   A common cause is the loss of a significant relationship to someone with whom the person has been close or attached. The more irredeemable the loss appears to be and the closer and more attached to the relationship one might have been tends to greatly influence the severity of the depression.

2.   The failure to obtain an important goal may trigger a depression. A good example is if one is trying to enter college, but fails to gain acceptance to any of the schools to which he or she has applied. An athlete may become quite depressed if he fails to be accepted into the professional ranks, or fails to receive an athletic scholarship. For children and young adults, it can be more common triggers such as the failure to gain a parent's approval for their accomplishments.

3.   A very key loss is that of losing a job. The loss of a job not only threatens one's self-esteem, but actually threatens the person's livelihood. Important abilities such as paying the rent and putting food on the table are threatened. An individual can become not only depressed, but anxious and, in some cases, even frightened. The loss of a job leads to the fourth agreed upon precipitating event which leads to depression, financial losses.

4.   If one loses money in the stock market or one's life savings is depleted because of a tragic event which had to be paid, depression may easily set in on the person. Safety and security are threatened. One may lose his place of residence. Financial status is lost.

5.   Another precipitating event is unexpected physical disability. A person can be injured in a traumatic accident, or be the victim of a devastating illness and lose abilities he previously had. The body may be weak and not able to do the physical things that it once did. The mind may be affected and intellectual abilities may be diminished or even absent. As a result, there is a tremendous impact on the person's life. Perhaps he or she can no longer work. He is not the same partner he was

to his spouse and cannot be the same parent to his children. There are a number of losses and how the person handles the loss can lead to or avoid depression.

6.   Many experts agree that a loss of social status can lead to depression. One may have the same relationship, for the most part. One may have the same husband or wife and many of the same friends, but once a person's reputation has been damaged, he or she does not have the same esteem or same acceptance in various circles he once had. An example would be a celebrity or actor who was once highly acclaimed with many awards. After making a number of poor choices in roles taken which give the actor terrible reviews, if it goes on long enough, the person may not be regarded as the same high-powered star he or she once was. If the person allows the regard of critics and peers to affect him or her, then the actor can become quite depressed.

In many professional circles, one's reputation not only is important for social receptions and invitations from one's peers, it actually affects business. If there is loss of social reputation, referrals and resources decline. All of it combines to trigger a depression.

In the dark night of the soul, there is a loss as well. However, it is hard to objectify the loss. Outwardly, nothing may appear different. The person is in good health, his significant other loves him, and there may be money in the bank. Outwardly, all may look well. People who see their friend would wonder, "What's wrong with him? Why is he so depressed? He has everything." What has been lost is a sense of spiritual fulfillment. The reason is something the person sometimes cannot identify. He does not experience the same joy from practiced spiritual activities. He may meditate, but there is no peace. He may pray, but feel as if his prayers are unheard. Even being in the company of like-minded spiritual individuals with whom he previously found joy may be unfulfilling. When that happens, the person may say to himself, "God has abandoned me." Nothing could be further from the truth. God is closer to that person that ever before.

However, the person has yet to realize that being spiritual is not a stagnant thing. One does not say, "I am spiritual" and remain the same the rest of his life. Life does change. It is also true of the spiritual path. The person, no matter how developed, must transform and grow as he lives his life. If one repeats the same action, if spiritual practices become a rote activity of going through the motions, there can be no fulfillment. Ernest Holmes, the founder of Religious Science, says, "We should remember that we have but started on an eternal ladder which ever spirals upwards."[5] The person who continues in a "sameness" regarding service to humanity and spirituality will ultimately reach a point of dissatisfaction. In the dark night, the loss is within, a loss of satisfaction from practices which no longer serve a person. The call is to go deeper into commitment and to continue to grow and transform in terms of consciousness and spirituality.

NOTE
1. Joel S. Goldsmith, *Consciousness is What I Am,* I-level Publications, Austell, Georgia, 1976, page 55.
2. Zechariah 4: 6.
3. Aaron T. Beck, MD, *Cognitive Therapy and Emotional Disorders,* Penguin Books, USA Inc., New York, NY, 1979, page 105.
4. Deuteronomy 6:5
5. Ernest Holmes, *Living the Science of Mind,* DeVorss & Company, Publisher, Camarillo, CA, 1984, page 47.

Chapter 3

PLUNGING DEEPER INTO THE SHADOWS

Maladaptive behaviors, beliefs, and attitudes which prolong and exacerbate depression and keep the soul in darkness.

In depression, there is a chain reaction of events. Following the precipitating event which is the loss, the person may try to reacquire what was lost, or if it is decided that the loss cannot be regained, make attempts to placate himself. If the attempts are unsuccessful, the depression deepens and the person begins to think worse of himself. With each unsuccessful attempt or each refusal to accept the loss, there is a downward spiral which seems to have no bottom. Therapy or some type of intervention which can interrupt the cycle is necessary. Insights and spiritual transformations may intervene as well.

One key observation is that everybody who suffers one of the significant losses does not become depressed. Also, there are innumerable unmentioned losses which can also lead to depression. What is the difference between a person who experiences a significant loss when something is taken from him and becomes depressed and one who does not? The difference is the meaning the loss has to the person who has lost it. A man who treasures his wife and dotes upon her and suddenly loses her companionship by death or separation will become severely depressed because he loved his wife greatly. She meant everything to him. On the other hand, a man who has a dissatisfying relationship with his spouse and has come to dislike her despite the many years they have been together may rejoice when she dies or leaves him. He may say to himself, "I'm glad she's gone. I was wondering how in the heck I was going to be rid of her." The meaning attached to the losses is quite different. One will lead to significant depression, and the other will lead to great joy. The man who losses his despised wife might throw a party after she has been gone for a period of time.

I am reminded of a scene I saw in a movie with Steve Martin, the renowned actor comedian. In the movie, he and his girlfriend were having problems. He met another woman in whom he became interested, but he was conflicted about it because of his relationship with his current girlfriend. When he went to see his present girlfriend, she started an intense angry argument. She blasted Steve Martin verbally and then slammed the door in his face thereby ending the relationship. Steve Martin turned away with his shoulders stooped and his head hung down to his chest. As he walked towards his car, it looked as if he was in deep mourning, but then his legs began to wiggle. At first, it looked as if he were going to fall, then his hands began to writhe and move, and it seemed as if he was in intense agony. Then, his feet began to dance, and he began to wave his arms wildly and to shout, "I'm free of my relationship." It was a hilarious moment for anyone watching the movie. In an instant, the viewer went from believing his relationship was extremely significant to him and that he was crushed, to realizing it was not significant at all and he was relieved to be free of his burden. The ending of his relationship with his girlfriend did not cause Steve Martin's character depression or mourning but instead elation and joy.

In the depression characteristic of the dark night, the loss is not worldly. Unlike common depressions caused by the deprivation of a material thing, in this case, the deprivation is of a spiritual nature. It could stem from disappointment with one's spiritual progress. As has been previously mentioned, one may consider himself a "back slider." A major concern is his relationship with God, a relationship in which the person finds himself wanting. The only resource that seems to truly help is any type of awareness of one's union with the Divine.

Another characteristic of depression is suicidal ideation.

When the pain becomes unbearable, the person believes that his or her life is hopeless. He or she can see no end to his or her suffering. In some depressions where the desired object has been lost, the thought is that it is not only irretrievable, but there is nothing that can ever replace it. The person incorrectly concludes that there is no point in living. Why shouldn't he just take himself out of the misery that is life? He or she views death as an escape from the emotional torture he or she is enduring. Death becomes more attractive than life.

As a psychiatry resident, I once had a middle-aged, Caucasian male patient on my caseload who was very depressed. He was so depressed that he required hospitalization at the Veterans Hospital where I was receiving my training. I established a very good, therapeutic relationship with him, and after he was discharged following the resolution of his depression, I followed him as an outpatient. Even with regular sessions and medication, he began to decompensate again and actually planned suicide. He had planned to go into his garage, lock the door, and turn on the car's engine. He picked the hour to do it while his wife was away at work. He called me to say goodbye. I immediately called his wife and asked her to look in on him and bring him to the hospital if need be. Her prompt actions saved his life and he was hospitalized. Following his second discharge, he and I discussed his suicide attempt and the rationale behind it. He engaged me in a heartfelt argument about his right to commit suicide. Although he was not suicidal at the time of our conversation, he was clearly able to show me how attractive an option suicide had been at the time he was feeling such despair. In addition, to him, it was the reasonable and rational thing to do. Fortunately, his life was saved by the intervention of his wife and I. When I left the outpatient service and the wards on which I was training, I followed him and at last contact, he was still in therapy.

A person who has entered the night of darkness also yearns to be free from a life of suffering. Such a person may desire death. However, since it is not the loss of worldly possessions which has caused his misery, at an intuitive level, the person knows that leaving the world is not the answer. Inner turmoil involves making peace within. The worse thought is that one is separate from God's love. The greatest desire is to know that love again. Although a person may feel hopeless and be filled with aches and despair, he is aware that killing himself would not bring him God's love. As a result, the idea is not very entertaining. One resolves, then, to continue to trod along his road and journey through the darkness. Although one cannot perceive it in one's depressed and disillusioned state, the love one seeks has never left him and never leaves him alone. The very thing he seeks is what leads him through the shadow of ignorance and error and into the light. The love he does not believe he has and which he seeks is the very element which motivates him.

To a person who is experiencing depression and to a spiritual seeker who is going through the dark night of the soul, the experience seems to last an eternity. Life seems hopeless to him and often he believes there is no tomorrow. In truth, the dawn is breaking in some near unforeseen future. However, there are a number of factors which can prolong the depression one is experiencing and lengthen the duration of the dark night through which he is passing.

One very important attitude which influences depression in an adverse manner is a sense of separation. The depressed person will conclude that he is all by himself in the world with his problem, and that there is no one who can help. Even if there is a loving family, an adoring wife or husband, or doting parents available to assist an individual, the person's perspective is he is going it alone. Unrealistically, he concludes that nobody cares. Again, the lyrics of the previously mentioned BB King blues song aptly describe the state, "Nobody loves me but my mama, and she could be jiving too."

In extreme cases, the sufferer may conclude that there is no help available from anyone, not even God. The spiritual seeker may even conclude that God has abandoned him. Not only is he separate from the Holy Spirit, but God no longer loves him. The despair and misery one feels when he reaches the previous conclusion is unbearable. It is when death becomes more attractive than life. The person going through depression then becomes suicidal. The spiritual seeker's need to turn within becomes greater. Both are immobilized. Hopelessness wins the day.

In order to proceed through depression and move through the shadow, it is necessary to overcome the sense of pervasive separation. It is the time for divine truth and the comfort of others. As one sees himself separate from everything, even God, the person who is suffering may not ask for assistance because he does not believe he deserves it. He feels unloved and unwanted. It behooves friends, family and caretakers to make an effort to assist the depressed individual. A simple truth, that God is everywhere in His fullness for God is omnipresent, may help a person realize that he can never be separate from the divine loving presence of the Almighty. It is now that is the time for the spiritual seeker to enter into the fellowship of kindred spirits. Until the sense of separation begins to dispel, there can be no exit from depression or darkness.

One of the most significant factors which prolong depression and dwelling in the shadows is denial. It is when a person truly cannot "see the forest for the trees." The oaks and pines of despair are all around him, but he cannot acknowledge that he has wandered deep into the woods. He cannot see that he has lost his way. Until he can admit it, he cannot find the path out of the wilderness. Psychotic individuals who are very paranoid are prime examples of people who live in denial. They blame everyone else for what happens to them and never can accept the truth of their own situation. They are the ones who define denial as "a river in African, somewhere in Egypt."

Depressive individuals who are languishing in their problem are rejecting the truth about their circumstance. They may be so depressed that they are numb and cannot really understand their true condition. More than likely, however, it is that they cannot accept a precipitating event, which led to their depression and the subsequent dark night of the soul.

A jilted lover may say, "Oh, she's not really gone. She'll be back," rather than accepting the truth that the beloved no longer cares and has moved out of his life. A spiritual seeker may be attached to a certain church, minister, or some tradition, for which a bond exists and deny that it no longer serves him and that he needs to move ahead with his life. The longer he continues to deny the process going on within him, the longer he will be depressed. Many people are aware that the spiritual process is dynamic and ever changing. We are constantly growing and being made new. However, many people fight the change. Paradoxically, they want to grow and become enlightened while remaining the same. It is impossible and will lead to stress.

For the jilted lover continuing to hold on to the person who has left him behind, it is in failing to accept the loss of the relationship that will lead to consequences and serious problems. He will not be able to find comfort in others who are very suitable for him. His pervasive sense of loss will keep him mired in depression. His ability to function will begin to diminish. In worse case scenarios, he will be unable to sleep or even eat and finally become suicidal.

Another way of living in denial is avoiding the situation. Avoidance is paramount in the case of individuals who suffer from phobias. People who have phobias, however, know the situation they want to avoid and take pains to avoid it. If their phobia is about heights or closed spaces, they avoid high places and tight quarters. In denial, the person simply says the situation does not exist, or it has no power over him. Affirming that something has no power over you is very good if it happens to be true. However, if the person has just lost a job, and after crying about it, instead of acknowledging the loss, they simply say, "Oh, it does not matter. I really did not like that job anyway," they are avoiding the situation. More than that, they are suppressing and minimizing their feelings.

Like many American men of my generation, I grew up watching movies of the late, legendary Hollywood cowboy and movie star John Wayne. In all of his films, John Wayne was a manly man. All the boys wanted to be tough and masculine like him, including me. One of the rules he lived by in his films was, "Big boys and men don't cry." No matter what happened in a film, he just took it, went out, and punched the bad guy. The message was clear. To be tough and strong like "the Duke," John Wayne, we had to suppress and minimize our feelings.

An entire generation of men has grown up suppressing and minimizing their feelings and the results have been broken homes, suicides, failed relationships, and lost opportunities. Women are given permission to cry and to show their feelings, much more so than men. However, even with women, if they continue to show their feelings about something, they are labeled a whiner or a crybaby. Even their friends might begin to avoid them. No matter what society labels a person, however, it is important that one accepts his feelings. It is unhealthy and even damaging for one to hold in his emotions which are clamoring to be dealt with and expressed. One's refusal to deal with pain, loss, or depression does not solve a problem, it only prolongs it. Denying the process will only allow it to continue until the pain is so great that the one who is suffering has a total collapse.

In a moment of creativity, some years ago while studying in ministerial school; I created a process for addressing psychological problems. It is a shorthand method for describing what therapists do all the time and what people who are successfully dealing with their problems do. I call it the AAA Program. The A's stand for: 1) Awareness, 2) Analysis, and 3) Action. I believe that the three elements are present in any plan, which we successfully utilize to address a situation or precipitating event leading to depression. Analyzing what is happening and deciding which factors are necessary to be changed and deciding what actions to take to correct the situation after analysis are extremely important. However, the most important single factor is first being aware that something is happening to you. Acceptance overcomes denial and moves into awareness.

There are a number of maladaptive behaviors, which are the actions which cause a person to move deeper into the wilderness of despair. One of the most popular maladaptive behaviors is drinking alcohol and the use of drugs. For a number of years, I have worked at a dual diagnosis clinic in Los Angeles. The people who come to the clinic are women who are seriously addicted to drugs and alcohol, and in addition also suffer from a major mental disorder. Some have been so seriously addicted to their drug of choice that they have given birth to children who underwent drug withdrawal at the time of birth. As a result, social agencies have taken the children from the women and have required them to go into treatment. In hopes of having their children returned to them, the women complied with the prescribed treatment.

When I see the aforementioned group of women as they come in for treatment, they often acknowledge their destructive behavior with illegal substances. The other diagnosis for many of them is major depression, often recurrent. In fact, a number of the women had such severe depressions it occasionally required hospitalization. When the persons experienced depression, rather than seek a solution to the problem, often they would turn to drugs. One woman told me, "Doctor, I had issues. I had to have marijuana every day just so I could deal." While she was under the influence of marijuana, she did not worry about her issues. Once she came out from under the influence of the drug, her issues still existed and triggered the recurring depression. As a result, she obtained more marijuana and became "stoned" again. She continued the cycle of becoming "high," becoming depressed, and then becoming "high" again, which led her life into a downward spiral.

Drugs only numb the pain. They do not remove the source of the hurt or agony. Using drugs to deal with issues only leads to a vicious cycle of agony. As uncomfortable as sobriety may be, it is still the best choice; and once sober, it is good to find a means of addressing the problem at hand. No matter how bleak it may look, there is always a divine solution.

A second maladaptive behavior which depressed people are prone to exhibit includes withdrawal and isolation from others. People who are severely depressed will withdraw and isolate themselves--even from very loving family members. Husbands will turn away from their wives. Wives will lock husbands out of the bedroom. Children will shun their parents. A friend will stay away from a friend. It is not that the love that was there has disappeared. The bond that was there before is still present. The person simply has very little energy to interact and no will to make the effort. As a result of the self-imposed isolation, the depression gets worse. Since the person is spurning all help, he makes the statement true that, "no one can help me." He first has to receive the help that is already there.

It is the time when the person most needs to be in the company of kindred spirits, people with good intentions and who have high minds. While there may be a strong urge to be alone, it is better to accept the company of those who have one's best interests at heart. Even if their efforts fall short, what is most important is to be in the presence of caring individuals. Spirit will be there in the midst of them and healing at some level will take place.

A third maladaptive factor is avoidant behavior. Avoidant behavior is especially true of extremely anxious individuals, especially people who are phobic or have panic disorder. It is still true, however, of people who are depressed. All of the individuals try to avoid the pain of situations with which they associate their depressive or anxious feelings. The problem with continuing avoidant behavior is the person who is phobic never overcomes his phobia. The person who has panic disorder remains panicked by the situation. The person who is depressed never confronts the cause of his depression. It is no surprise then that the person remains ill. He rationalizes it by telling himself, "It's too much for me," or "there's nothing I can do about it," and other similar excuses.

Avoidance is more true of a simple or plain depression than of someone who is depressed and also in the dark night of the soul. The spiritual seeker knows that he or she cannot avoid what is happening to him or her, so the person surrenders to the process after a period of time. At some level, he or she knows that one has to go through the fire to be cleansed. The person who is simply experiencing depression and has not reached the insight of the spiritual seeker may decide that there is some way he can avoid addressing the problem or situation and still become no longer depressed. It is not the case.

In a psychiatric practice, people are sometimes given minor tranquilizers in order to allay their anxiety causing it to be sufficiently mild, so that they can enter a very anxiety-provoking situation which they would usually avoid. When used to help confront a problem, the role of minor tranquilizers is very good. By diminishing the anxiety, the person can speedily face the situation; ultimately, if they are given the tranquilizers simply to get rid of the anxiety and the stressor is not addressed, tranquilizers will work against a person's progress.

It is a good idea for family members and health practitioners to remember that it is extremely difficult for the depressed or anxious individual to confront a situation. The expectation that he would immediately come face-to-face with his problem and fight through it is unrealistic. Often, it takes months before a person can build up the nerve or find a means of handling his anxiety to the point where he can address the conflicting situation. Also, many times supportive personnel and objects are necessary to give him the assistance he needs. All that really matters is that he moves in the direction of actually addressing his situation and not run from it.

Still, another maladaptive behavior is blaming others and avoiding personal responsibility. It is the self defense of paranoid individuals and people who want to look good to protect their self image and avoid examining their own faults by putting the blame squarely on someone else's shoulders. Immature individuals will often engage in this type of behavior. Engaging in blaming behavior prevents growth and healing. Also, it pushes away people who would otherwise come to one's aid. The spiritual seeker is unlikely to engage in blaming as he goes through the dark night of the soul. He is busy examining himself and trying to find out what did he do to lose God's favor as he or she may perceive it. He is busy examining how he laid himself so low. Meanwhile, the person who is paranoid and mired in depression may say to himself, "It's his fault or her entire fault. If they had done this, or if they had done that, I would be alright." The statements have no place in the healing process and have to be discarded. The immaturity and blame must be replaced with acceptance of personal responsibility for one's actions. It is the hallmark of the mature individual and the spiritual soul to accept responsibility for the things they do. More important, it is a sign of both psychological and spiritual health. Accepting the ownership of one's actions gives one dominion over his or her world. It is not what someone else does, but what the individual does that creates his reality.

Ownership and personal responsibility overcomes blame and allows a person to become active in transforming his life for the good. A negative action which is related to blaming others is that of accusing others and being verbally or physically aggressive towards them. People who blame others for their problems will often threaten them, and then they wonder why the person is avoiding them. In their depression or anxiety, they cannot see the harm they are doing. Often, it has to be pointed out by others. When a person cannot see the harm he is doing, he feels entitled to make threats because, after all, isn't that other person the one who is responsible for his problems? The person may think, "Why shouldn't I threaten him and make him do what I want him to do?" He attacks and abuses others, both verbally and physically, with a righteous wrath and anger, although, truth be told, depressed people are usually too depressed to become mad at anybody. They are just too busy being depressed. However, in their depression, they can be very accusatory; not the best way to win friends and influence people, especially when you need them. Again, it is a way of fulfilling the statement, "No one wants to help me. There is no one who can help me." It is true because the person is running them away.

Therefore, sometimes it is necessary to just sit down and think. The person may ask, "What is it that I'm doing to people to push them out of my life?" One does not assume that he or she is a bad human being or has a major personality deficit. It is simply something that he or she is doing which needs to be corrected. The depressed individual has to be taught to thank people for whatever they may do, no matter how small, when they do something for them in their depression. It helps them to move away from accusing others. He needs to be helped in praising people rather than accusing them, and particularly, he needs to be assisted in praising himself. If the person is receptive to a new attitude of praising others and thanking them for whatever small act they may do, he or she is well on the road to recovery. Spiritual seekers, as they turn away from accusation and begin to move into some semblance of an attitude of gratitude are beginning to walk out of the forest of despair and darkness. As they stop accusing others and accept them for the spiritual beings that they are, they not only begin to move out of depression, but they begin to move into their own spiritual heritage.

A sixth action which keeps the soul in depression and darkness is excessively blaming oneself. It is the flip side of the coin of blaming others. It is distinguished from accepting personal responsibility in that personal responsibility allows a person to mobilize and take action on his situation. Excessive blaming stops a person from making an effort. He or she becomes immobilized and can do nothing. He or she is unable to see factors which led to the situation that have very little or perhaps nothing to do with him or herself. He or she is the one who sings the songs, "Woe is me," "Everything happens to me," or "It is my fault, and now I cannot do anything about it." Yes, it is true that we all have a part to play in the problems we create for ourselves. However, it is also true that everything is not our fault. A misfortune that happens to a friend which causes us to be depressed may not have anything to do with anything that we did. The wife or husband who left may have done so because they wanted to leave and there is no need for the person who is left behind to blame him or herself because of the other person's actions. The problem with excessive blaming is that the person who is doing it loses all objectivity. He or she cannot see where what someone else does ends and what he or she is doing begins.

In a dark night of the soul, the spiritual seeker sees himself as a debased sinner with no redeeming qualities and completely forgets about the saving grace of God. Psychologically, it is the time to remember that all people have free choice, and what someone else does, no matter how we perceive it, may not have anything to do with us. We can move out of blame and allow other people to take control of their lives. We remember that people have the freedom to choose to take actions which they want to take, whether we like them or not. The person who is blaming himself for everything moves into the victim role when he allows actions that others take to determine his destiny. It sets the script for the rest of his life. An assumption might be, "My wife left me. I wasn't a good enough husband. She's the only person I've ever loved, so I'm doomed to be alone for the rest of my life." He is now the victim of his wife who left him. He has decided to suffer until he dies. There is no need to become such a victim. There is no need to blame himself and remain in pain because she decided to leave.

Another aspect we need to remember is that although we are indeed responsible for our own actions, we are not responsible for unforeseen tragic events. Recently, I was watching a movie on television. In the film, the principal actor, Jennifer Lopez, was guilt-ridden about an automobile accident in which her husband died. She had fallen asleep at the wheel, but both of them had decided together to keep driving late at night. They were trying to reach a destination before morning came. They flipped a coin and it was her turn to drive while he slept. Inadvertently, at 3:30 a.m., she fell asleep, and before they knew it, the car had overturned. He was killed, but she lived and then blamed herself, in this story, for what had happened to him. She continually blamed herself for his death, and it caused her to have no end to her grief.

They made a bad decision, but they made it together. That she fell asleep could just as easily have been him falling asleep. There was no one to blame. It was a bad decision on both their parts and an unfortunate accident. However, she became involved in excessive blame, could not dismiss it, and the character was led into a profound depression. It helps to remember that the world does not revolve around us, and we do not control everything. In fact, sometimes it is hard enough to simply control ourselves let alone assume total responsibility for an unfortunate depressive event. It is not only unrealistic, sometimes it even borders on the ridiculous. Even more so, the spouse or lover who allows a decision or action made by his or her ex-partner to determine the rest of his or her life is indeed a victim. However, he or she is not a victim of that person's actions. The person is a victim of his own decision. Once he decides there is something that he can do, once he perceives that he is not helpless and can make a change, change comes. Whether it is a person or a situation, it makes no difference. The result is the same. One then sets foot on the path out of the vale of shadow.

Finally, the seventh maladaptive maneuver--one of my favorites--has often been defined as "insanity." It is the act of repeating the same action and expecting different results. It is just like mixing up ingredients which make a cake yet expecting to make bread. You will make a cake every time. That is often what we do. We keep repeating the same actions over and over again, and wonder if somehow it will be different this time. The answer is no, it will not. It will be the same as it was before. The reason we keep doing it is because it is a repetitive action which brings temporary relief, but it does not bring any solution. We seek the relief. We want a break from the anxiety or depression, so we repeat what we have done. We go to see the person who we know we are not supposed to see because we find a respite there. However, after we leave him or her, we have the same problem. It is similar to an obsessive compulsive disorder where the person becomes overcome with anxiety and the fear of germs, so he goes and washes his hands and immediately he is relieved. Soon thereafter, the urge returns, and he repeats his behavior. The hand washing will bring relief, but again the urge and the fear returns.

The solution is diligent work to change the obsessive thought pattern. The easiest action to take is to repeat the hand washing again, but we find the same result and no solution. People who experience depression will ruminate and return to old habits. The repetitive behavior is addictive because it does bring some relief. However, it is ultimately unsatisfying. The spiritual seeker who is on the journey through the night finds no satisfaction in what he used to do. The rituals which served him or her before no longer are fulfilling. To begin to resolve depression and to move to the next phase of spiritual evolution, one must try something new. It is best if there is an intuitive moment of insight and inspiration. It is Spirit's way of revealing the new direction. It is the mind having arrived at a new conclusion. It is important that the person follows what has been revealed. Often, however, nothing comes. When one seems stuck, he can be patient, but it is important to be patient with an open mind and an active imagination, which is constantly seeking a solution. Often, it is better just to try something, even if it is wrong. One learns from the mistake, and through trial and error he begins to find his way.

There are a number of false assumptions and negative thoughts which serve as the rationale for maintaining maladaptive behaviors. If the destructive beliefs are maintained, not only will they keep the individual in darkness, they will move him further into despair. All the while, the one who is suffering accepts the maladaptive thought as a fact. It is not a fact; it is only a distorted opinion. The truth is that the statements have very little basis in reality. One of the biggest thought patterns which keep an individual in depression and immobilizes him as he treads along the spiritual path is the thought pattern of helplessness. For some reason, the individual believes that he will fail at anything he tries. In fact, often the person will actually believe it is pointless to even try. Here, he says, "I'm helpless. There is nothing I can do. It wouldn't matter anyway." To accept such arguments as truth causes a person to lose dominion over his life. The outcome is withdrawal and seclusion. The individual is paralyzed and inactive. Self-empowerment has to be realized somewhere along the journey in order to move out of depression and to move forward into spiritual progress.

Another false assumption which is akin to helplessness and is just as destructive is that of hopelessness. Here, again the person says there is no point in doing anything. However, the reason is not because he or she cannot do anything, but the individual concludes that no matter what he may do, it will not work out. So, the person reiterates what his helpless cousin says by saying, "There's no point in doing anything." In some ways, the stance of hopelessness is actually worse than helplessness. When there is hope, a person may be encouraged to persevere. Even though he is helpless, there is a possibility that some miracle will see him through the situation. It is not the case when a person yields to hopelessness. It is all over at that point. In fact, when all hope leaves, that is when suicide becomes the only option. The spiritual seeker may consider things as hopeless, but if he or she is sincere, the fundamental belief in all religions that with God all things are possible will penetrate the distorted belief and dispel it into the nothingness from which it came. It will vanish and be dissolved.

The spiritual seeker may think that as a human being he is hopeless, but even in the darkest hour the belief that God's grace can work miracles and can rescue him from the deepest pit is somewhere present. That alone, if acknowledged, is enough to dispel hopelessness. It is what keeps a person pushing forward along his path. Without the spiritual aspect, there is only profound depression and suicide is a real danger. It is at that point when the therapist has to really question the irrational conclusions which the person has reached. The person is using emotional reasoning. The situation is hopeless because it "feels hopeless." The truth is that he simply has a conviction that it is hopeless. He has a strong opinion, a very firm belief that it is hopeless. However, it is still just his opinion. There are other opinions and there are other convictions. Occasionally when bombarded with evidence to the contrary, the depressed person has to give up his stance of hopelessness.

Yet another false assumption which forms a basis for actions and attitudes which keep a person in shadow and despair is catastrophic thinking. It is akin to one's "making a mountain out of a molehill." No matter what the person does for a situation, he believes his actions will only make it much worse than it already is. The individual engaged in catastrophic thinking concludes that every outcome will be negative. His mantras are "I'm only going it make it worse," and "The worst is going to happen." Even when a person takes an action and it has a degree of success, he sees it through a filter where the good part of an action is minimized and any imperfections are the parts upon which he focuses. The person ends up feeling overwhelmed. He has a sense of impending doom. It is necessary for the soul to apply a degree of perspective, so it may know that the task before it can be managed.

A final maladaptive belief to consider which serves as a foundation for destructive deeds which prolong the dark night are the thoughts of self-criticism and deficiency. Not only does the person believe that he is defective, he believes that someone else has the solution to his problems. He feeds himself thoughts such as, "I'm no good," and "if only so-and-so loved me, everything would be alright." Overcoming self-criticism and poor self-esteem can be a major chore in psychotherapy. The spiritual seeker who sees himself as a no good, backsliding sinner may need to dwell on the grace and forgiveness of God, as well as his own innate worth and value as a child of God.

There is one final consideration which is maladaptive to progress. The person who is depressed and living as though in the darkness tends to see more depression and darkness. He has a type of tunnel vision, but he is honing in only on the problem that is presenting itself to him. As he pays attention to the problem, he comprehends more of the problem. He goes deeper into the forest of despair, and in his consciousness, he falls further away from the divine union that he seeks. I am reminded of the scripture which reads: "I will lift up mine eyes to the hills from whence cometh my help."[1] Metaphorically, it means look away from that which is pulling you down. Raise your vision above the mundane and the desperate. Raise your vision and look at what it is that is bringing you wholeness--look at what is benefiting you. The test, then, is to move one's eyes away from the problem and to look at the solution. Although the solution may not be immediately apparent, it is a shift in consciousness which needs to take place. In looking unto the hills from whence cometh its help, the soul is actively seeking options which may work to help benefit it and raise its awareness.

NOTE
1. Psalms 121:1

Chapter 4

Awareness and Acceptance

The beginning steps in overcoming depression and moving towards the light.

Depression is a formidable adversary. It is a painful emotional state that can paralyze a person who suffers from it. When in its throes, one's life comes to a screeching halt. There is virtually no progress in any area, including spiritual growth. It follows, then, the first step an individual has to take in order to move through the dark night of the soul is to deal with the accompanying depression. It is a necessary requirement. The first step in overcoming depression is becoming aware. Before anyone can address his depression, he must know that he is depressed. Awareness is essential. Many people are depressed and do not even realize it. They go through life thinking, "That's just the way it is. Life's a drag." The sky to them is always grey and filled with storm clouds. Yet, they think it is a normal perspective. They do not realize that others see blue skies and sunshine. Often, persons will complain of being unable to sleep or having a poor appetite, and think it is all that is wrong, never stopping to realize that it is only one part of a much greater problem.

Awareness is the key. If someone thinks that something about him is different, it would be wise to consider that he may be depressed. When one does not feel the same, his body feels leaden, and he is just not himself and yet do not have any physical explanation for it, he has to turn within and ask, "What am I feeling?" If a feeling of sadness and dysphoria emerges, one can affirm that he is depressed. It is in being consciously aware that he is depressed that the individual takes the first step towards resolving the situation and overcoming the dark night.

Another important ingredient of awareness is knowing the process associated with resolving depression. It helps to know the nature of depression and what can be expected. Depression is a multi-factorial entity. It has many causes which lead to its experience and expression. Disappointing and even traumatic experiences contribute to the cause of depression, as well as a genetic or biological predisposition. Familial factors, such as having very close relatives who suffer from depression and being part of a family in which it has a high incidence can make a person sensitive to becoming depressed. Illness is a major factor in causing depression, as well as a maladaptive lifestyle, which can create or prolong the situation. Depression can be mild or it can be very severe. One can suffer only a few symptoms such as poor concentration or mild fatigue, or it can be as extreme as a persistent preoccupation with suicide and having to be hospitalized for safety's sake.

Depression leads to a downward spiral and people often do not think they can overcome it, but the truth is they can. The process of depression is such that after it sets in, the sufferer continues on a descending staircase and suffers from many symptoms, such as anorexia, insomnia, weakness, etc., until he or she reaches a point where there is a determination to improve. A complicated grieving can lead to prolonged depression. In the case of grief, crying, heavy sighing, and periods of intense gloom can be expected because one has lost something precious, a loved one has passed. It is healthy to release one's feelings and to express them. Despite society's pressure to recover from it quickly, it truly takes two years to recover sufficiently from the loss of a loved one. All of the anniversaries of birthdays, holidays, and special occasions have to be experienced with the dearly departed person being absent. Usually, once they have been experienced the second time, matters are resolved. If one's life cannot go on without the departed, one has moved to depression which may require clinical treatment. Loss is, in fact, the central theme of all depression. Something is lost. It is the sense of self, a loved one, a job, physical abilities or something. Cognitive therapists refer to it as "subtracting from his domain."[1] The perception is that the personal domain has been diminished. As one moves through the process of depression, he or she begins to realize that that which has been lost or diminished can be restored or replaced. In fact, it may never have been lost at all.

After becoming aware of his condition, the person who is depressed has a formidable task ahead of him. It can be very daunting and cause him to wish it would go away and others to try to pretend that it is not there. I am reminded of the opening scene from each episode of the old television series "Mission Impossible." It begins with a tape recorded message telling the secret agent, "Your mission, should you choose to accept it," and afterwards, the assignment would be described. Similarly, in dealing with depression, the situation has to be accepted.

Following awareness, the next most important step is acceptance. The sufferer has to accept the situation for just what it is. To pretend it is not so or to wish it away does absolutely nothing to facilitate acceptance. To ignore it is likened to denying the existence of the "800 pound gorilla" which is sitting in your living room. It continues to do damage. It continues to obstruct one's life, and causes dysfunction in: work, relationships, and all areas of living. Until depression is accepted and addressed, life can neither improve nor spiritual growth occur. As important as it is to acknowledge and accept a depressive state, it is just as important to keep from overemphasizing it or over-blowing it. I reiterate that a person must accept the situation for what it is. That means, not less than it is, or trying to ignore it completely, but also not to make it more than it is. When a person is in the throes of depression, every little action or event can become blown out of proportion. The depression which has been accepted may not look like an "800 pound gorilla" but like a "ten ton dinosaur." Again, the condition must be accepted for what it is but no more than that. It is a problem which one can address.

It is a challenge which must be met. The situation is evaluated objectively. If the depressed person cannot do it himself, then someone may need to help him evaluate it in a realistic manner. Once seen clearly, the circumstances of which one has been made aware becomes a challenge which can be met.

Clinicians, therapists, and spiritual counselors will advocate accepting the pain that is involved. Spiritual counselors will even urge the person who is suffering to be a disciple of the pain. The premise here is that there is a lesson in the situation somewhere. The pain of the depression is pointing out something to the person who is experiencing it and is, in essence, teaching him something. In fact, until the lesson is learned, the thought is that the pain will endure. So, the questions become, "What is the pain of the depression trying to teach one? What is it trying to warn you about?" In partnership with counselors, therapists, friends or whomever the person may choose, a search can be embarked upon to find an answer to the questions which have been raised. The questions cannot be asked and the search cannot begin until depression has been accepted. As the situation is both accepted and attended to, then growth begins. The kind of growth will depend on the particular situation of the individual, the choices he has to make, and the work he has to do. The only way pass the depressive situation is to accept the problem and then work through it.

Once acceptance takes place, then solutions will come to the person if he is genuinely interested in moving through the depression and overcoming the darkness of the soul. The person is to seek solutions with an open mind, and if he does, he will gain insights from the suffering as the solutions come.

We have in our world literature great examples of people who dealt with depression. We know of key figures, especially in our spiritual traditions, who dealt with turmoil and despair yet triumphed. No greater ones come to mind than Jesus The Christ and The Buddha. They accepted their pain and gained insight and strength from it. They suffered greatly, were transformed, and eventually transformed the entire world. They are good examples for the rest of us. Their stories are metaphors for how we, once we are aware of our depressive circumstances, can accept it, embrace it, experience insights and "ah ha's," and move into a greater expression of life. Jesus The Christ accepted his dire circumstance when he entered the Garden of Gethsemane. He was keenly aware of his pain, which was vividly described in Luke 22:44 where it says, "And being in an agony, He prayed more earnestly and his sweat was as it were great drops of blood falling down to the ground." Yet and still, he found the courage and strength to move through his turmoil and embrace his destiny and fulfill the purpose for which he was born. Jesus The Christ transcended his turmoil, embraced his inner divinity, and ultimately transformed all of humankind as he accepted his fate by saying in Luke 22:42, "Father, if thou be willing, remove this cup from me. Nevertheless, not my will but thy will be done."

Even before Jesus The Christ lived and gave his great example to the world, there was another before him, Siddhartha Gautama whose life illustrated the importance of acceptance and surrender in overcoming despair and growing spiritually. Siddhartha Gautama, The Buddha, became known as "The Enlightened One." He lived 500 years before Christ in India. He was born a prince, but a wise man told his father, the king, while Siddhartha was but an infant that the son would not follow the father and become a ruler, but would become a world savior. Although his father tried to immerse Siddhartha in pleasure and distractions, as he matured the prince became concerned with the problem of suffering and wanted to understand the true meaning of human life. He practiced severe austerities trying to find answers, but failed. He was desperate in his longings. Although feeble from his efforts, he made one final determination when he sat underneath a huge fig tree and declared, "Blood may become exhausted, flesh may decay, bones may fall apart, but I will never leave this place until I find the way to enlightenment."[2] With that statement, the one who was to become The Buddha surrendered all that he was to his next stage of evolution and accepted his situation. He was determined to attain his goal, even if it meant his death. Various texts try to describe the experiences and insights he received as he sat in turmoil underneath the bodhi tree. After a long life-threatening, nightmarish night, he found the way to enlightenment.

A vital element which can help a person to overcome depression and also is a part of accepting life for what it is is having a warrior mentality. By that, I do not mean going out and looking for something to fight or with which to engage in combat or conflict. Instead, I am referring to a stance that many people who are depressed do not take. The cognition is such that the person thinks of himself as a victim and in a sense becomes one. "Woe is me." "There is nothing I can do" only further fuels the depression and causes him to spiral further downward in terms of his self image and well being. The warrior not only actively accepts the condition but takes a stand and decides to meet the challenge; he is neither inert nor inactive. The warrior actively addresses the situation. Thus, a challenge to one person may be a catastrophe to another when considering the warrior mentality. Some people may have more inner tools with which to resolve a certain situation than others. They may have more constitutional fortitude. Whatever the case may be, ultimately, somewhere deep within, the person has to decide to take a stand regardless of resources or innate talents and abilities. As the challenge is met, a person is often surprised to uncover the resources he finds within himself and in his environment. The discoveries boost his self-esteem and interrupt the downward spiral, so that he begins to move through the forest of darkness and begins once more to walk along the path towards the light. The traumatic event is no longer viewed as a disaster. The gauntlet has been thrown and the event is viewed as a challenge. As the warrior mentality is acquired, the concept of victim-hood is slowly discarded. The person no longer looks at himself as a victim, but as someone who can actively influence and change his life. As one meets the challenge, he will ultimately find that it is truly an opportunity to learn, evolve, and grow.

Another factor that is very important in having the assertive attitude that is necessary to accept one's circumstance and overcome depression is being willing to take the actions necessary to correct the situation. As one appraises his situation, even realistically, it can be rather intimidating. It can easily appear to be too much to overcome and an individual can decide that the sacrifice is too great to try to cope with the problem. The decision that one makes concerning acceptance is the necessary key to bring about change. However, in order to overcome, one must not only be willing to meet the challenge, action must be taken. It is at this key juncture that the individual decides, if he is to overcome, not only to have a warrior mentality but to become a master. No longer is he helpless to do anything about his crisis. By making the decision to make whatever sacrifices are necessary and to take whatever actions are needed, he mentally takes control of his circumstance. It is said that as god-beings we have dominion. It means more than dominion over the creatures of the earth as it says in the Bible. It means we have dominion over our lives, over ourselves, and over our personal world. When we are depressed we give up dominion. Of course, it only drives us further into darkness and despair. However, we always have dominion. We only have to decide to reclaim our heritage. When we decide to move forward in action, become the master, and claim dominion over our lives, we are on the road to well-being.

Another important part of acceptance which helps overcome depression is honesty concerning our feelings and emotions. As we acknowledge the circumstances or events that have caused us to become depressed, we are assailed with unpleasant emotions. There is "wailing and gnashing of the teeth." In the face of such misery, it is only natural to try to turn away from what is perceived as the cause of the depression. However, in accepting our condition and overcoming it, we not only acknowledge our feelings, we give vent to them, and we express them. As in the case of someone who is undergoing grief concerning the loss of a loved one, the feelings have to be released. Nevertheless, we are not victimized by those feelings, but we are there with them. We acknowledge the aching in our bones. We accept the pain in our hearts; the agony we feel in our body and in the depth of our beings. We are with the feeling. We are present in the here and now with what is happening with our emotions. We observe the ebb and the flow of our feelings and, as we deal with them, we gain strength.

An additional factor in overcoming depression is that of patience. Patience is more than just a virtue, it is a vital resource which demonstrates perseverance and tolerance to endure and eventually overcome an obstacle in one's life. When a person is truly depressed, every day feels like an eternity. He sighs and wonders when his torment will end. It seems as if there will never be any relief. People who enter treatment often want instant results. They want to be well right now. It is easy to understand how they feel; however, the expectation is unrealistic. Initially, I would tell anyone who entered into treatment with me during my private practice that it would take time to resolve the disorder. Working in psychotherapy may take months or even years to truly bring lasting benefits. When psychotherapy alone is not enough or when medication is what is truly indicated, even people who respond to a particular medicine may take weeks before they begin to feel better. There is no way to avoid it. It takes time to move through the darkness and depression. It is important that the ones who are helping those who are dwelling in the shadow to let them know that life will improve. Clinically, depression has a good prognosis. Statistics show that a high percentage of people do improve and are then able to move forward with their lives. Before the morning comes, however, one first has to endure the long, dark night, and that requires patience.

In coping with pain and despair, one may need to be fully

present, not just to the suffering but in order to bring forth all the resources at one's disposal to be triumphant. Therefore, a person practices "being present" from moment-to-moment and not just from day-to-day. Tears may be flowing like a flood one minute, but relief may come in the next. It is good to be aware of both and to experience both completely. Patience is aided by the knowledge that the pain that is being experienced is not permanent. It will peak and seem intolerable, but then it will fall away. Most importantly, it will not last. Patience is embraced and encouraged. The quality of patience requires an element of faith which reassures the sufferer that if he perseveres, life may not be as he desires, but eventually, it will be alright.

After one has become aware of his depression and gains the knowledge that he may be moving through a dark time filled with dread and despair, he may also come to accept his condition for what it is without making it seemingly worse or making light of it. Then, the next step that the individual has to take is deciding how to address the situation. It is indeed the crucial step. One can become aware of his situation and even be very accepting of it, and yet still decide to take no action. In the discussion of acceptance which we have just had, perspective and insight were intended to give the individual inspiration to meet his challenge. The idea is to let the person know that in becoming aware of his circumstance and in accepting it with understanding; he is now equipped to handle it. He can now find the means to cope with and overcome his happenstance.

NOTE
1. Aaron T. Beck, MD, *Cognitive Therapy and the Emotion Disorders,* Penguin Books, USA, Inc., New York, NY, 1979, pg 58.
2. Bukkyo Dendo Kykai, *The Teachings of the Buddha,* Fifteenth edition, Kenkyusha Printing Co., Tokyo, Japan, 1971, pg 8.

Chapter 5

ANALYSIS AND ACTION

Identifying false ideas, destructive acts, painful patterns and correcting them with adaptive measures which restore cheer, well-being, and journey in the direction of the dawn.

There are a number of corrective measures which can be used to vanquish depression and despair. There is also a sequence which seems to be naturally followed as the person handles his problems. However, the sequence is not set and one stage may not necessarily precede the other. Corrective measures will be described here in what would be considered a logical sequence.

The initial measure requires identifying the precipitating or stressful event which traumatized the person and led him into depression and darkness. With awareness comes knowledge and with knowledge one can reflect on what has happened to him and begin to examine the preceding events. Usually, there is a pivotal event which caused such trauma that it can be identified as the time when everything began to spiral downward. It can be practically any event. What is important is how it affected the person to whom it happened. It can be as traumatic as the death of a loved one, or as simple as a devastating thought or insight which has never occurred before. Once it has been experienced, the soul is in torment. However, after identifying the precipitating or stressful traumatic event, through awareness, reflection, and examination of what has happened, the next step is to see what the actions or decisions were that one took or made to cause matters to worsen. It is important to determine how one reacted to the trauma. In so doing, the person needs to identify the false assumptions and maladaptive behaviors he used at that time to address the situation but which did not serve him and only caused a continual deterioration. As one looks back over the past, sometimes he will ask himself, "What was I thinking? What made me do that? Couldn't I see that that would only cause more trouble?" When it happens, the person is ready to identify the false assumption or maladaptive behavior that not only prolonged the condition but oftentimes caused it to become worse. Interestingly enough, usually at the time the behavior was employed, it seemed sensible. The person would have felt as if it were the correct behavior to express or exhibit. Also, often the initial thoughts which one had to appraise the condition also seemed to make sense, no matter how illogical they may appear upon reexamination. Thoughts can be simple assumptions, such as "It happened because I'm a loser," which might be some people's explanation for the occurrence. Another explanation which is irrational but which may have seemed logical at the time is the belief that, "Terrible events always happen to me." Ineffective coping may be explained by saying, "It's hopeless. There's no use in trying." All are false assumptions which lead to inertia, inaction, and agony.

An adaptive assumption when those kinds of thoughts are identified would be to think of oneself as a winner and not as a loser. We are divine beings. We have been given the gift of choice, which raises us above the animals. Our reasoning and ability to make choices means that we are losers only if we decide to be losers. We can just as easily and more effectively decide that we are winners, and life is for us. In fact, it is. Any human parent wants only the best for his or her child. God, the All Good, wants much more for His children. As a result, each person can be sure that the universe is for him; it is for her. Therefore, what we are in truth are winners, and any time we choose we can cast aside the notion that we are losers and that our efforts to make our life better are worthless. As we cast aside the self-criticism, we can embrace the truth that we are worthwhile individuals. It is a spiritual truth and a psychological fact. It is only our misconceptions which make it seem otherwise.

Now, having identified the false assumptions and maladaptive behaviors, one can replace them with rationale assumptions which are in tune with spiritual truth and psychological fact. One can also then begin to look for behaviors and actions which serve him, causes his life to improve, and move into a greater expression of well being.

As the false assumptions and maladaptive behaviors are identified and dissected, a person can begin to see the symptoms that they cause. The erroneous conclusions and destructive responses which came from the troublesome thoughts become clear. The destructive acts which are the direct results of acting on misguided thinking are pinpointed. Having identified the traumatic event and the distorted conclusions along with the destructive behaviors which were formed, one can now describe the results and symptoms of those thoughts and behaviors in detail. Now a person can really begin to take charge of his life. Each symptom and behavior can be evaluated as to how it adds or subtracts from ones general well being. It is the time to act. It is the time to construct new, more adaptive thoughts, and more adaptive ways of functioning in the world. As rational thoughts which are in tune with spiritual truth and psychological principles are explored and developed, the individual's attitude will change. By dwelling on the more beneficial thoughts which provide and sustain a more wholesome mental atmosphere, eventually a better attitude towards himself and life will take place. He will begin to think differently and as he does, he will feel differently. Cognitions which appraise his situations and actions, but do not distort them, especially in an adverse matter, will begin to be the way of thinking.

For many people, reaching the point of constructing new thoughts and behaviors is very difficult. Often, it is easier to stay mired in the muddy cognition in which they have dwelled so long. To deny the new perceptions which have been revealed, however, is also to refuse to move towards the light. It is to decide to remain in depression and in darkness. There is something within us, however, which wants to seek the light. There is also a cognitive dissonance which takes place when one knows what is best to do but then refuses to do it. The sincere seeker and the one who truly wants to be whole eventually must and will embrace the new thought constructs and the new adaptive behavior which they have discovered. The dark deeds and distorted thinking will be left behind. Therefore, both growth and change can begin to take place.

Having discovered new, more adaptive thoughts and behaviors, it is time to try new measures. Spiritually, it is known that faith must be accompanied by deeds. The doing of good deeds is one way in which faith is demonstrated. Likewise, in psychology, it is known that no matter how much insight one may have into a particular challenge, without an effort to confront and solve the situation, the insight is useless. An intellectual understanding of the new adaptive thoughts and behaviors is indeed a fine development. Until the person employs the new way of thinking and acting into his life, it is of no importance. As the new measures are incorporated into the person's experience and are used on a daily basis, an emotional change will take place with each success. He will become much less depressed and will begin to think better of himself. The new measures must be tried. When they are, with each step along the way out of the wilderness of shadow and sorrow, one will begin to feel the emergence of a feeling of joy. Even if it only occurs for a moment, there will be a fleeting glimpse of what is possible. The promise of the dawn is realized.

As previously unused or unknown methods are utilized and previously unrealized attitudes are acquired, the result received from putting them into action will vary. Success is not guaranteed whenever something is tried. What is important is that the effort is made. When one tries something new and it is not successful, it is important not to become discouraged, but to learn from what was tried. The seeker then begins to find others who are along the path with him, or who have gone before. The mind has to be kept open and the person who is overcoming depression needs to continue to realize that he can receive knowledge, not only from his mentors, but from anyone. It is imperative to be open to feedback concerning the actions which have been tried and to the thoughts and attitudes which have been retained. It helps one to discard ideas and beliefs which are useless and to utilize tools and practices which are going to be important in improving one's life. The ego is set aside. One is humbled and receptive to whatever is going to be of help, no matter from whom or from where it comes. When an action is ineffective, it is good to sit and reflect on what it was that needed to be done instead. The method which failed is analyzed and dissected, and a new, more effective method is chosen. Actions, thoughts and deeds are revised and adjusted until a new way is created that truly serves the individual and helps him along his journey.

If the measures and thoughts which a person tries, after having constructed new thoughts and behaviors are successful, it is truly wonderful. The seeker is to be congratulated and given encouragement. He can continue to use the successful measures. Even when the measures are successful, they are subject to refinement. What is learned from unsuccessful measures may be utilized in making adjustments because even the things which have not worked can sometimes be revised until something is found which does. Either way, the person will eventually succeed. I love the chant which many of us learned as children, "If at first you don't succeed, try and try again." It is so simple, and yet, so true. The one who is overcoming depression and spiritual darkness needs to be persistent. He will find the new thoughts and ways of being in the world that will work for him. If they make him begin to feel good and live in a productive, functional manner, the new ways and thoughts are to be continued. From time to time, they may be revisited, so that one will do even better. It is important to be persistent, to try and try again. One's success is assured, eventually there will be success, although it may not be clear what is necessary to be done initially, or even some time later as one moves through a depressive state.

As one seeks to employ corrective measures and to become more whole emotionally and spiritually, it is time to begin problem-solving. It is wise, both alone and with a trusted helper, to make a list of problems which need to be solved and the goals which one wants to reach. It is best to keep the list short at first and the solutions many. Now is the moment to do brainstorming. In so doing, possible solutions to the perceived depressive circumstances can be found. Brainstorming is defined as rapidly generating a series of possible solutions without evaluation or judgment. It can be extremely helpful in finding the corrective measures one needs to move forward. After setting initial goals and generating a list of problems which need to be solved, one can begin to generate solutions. It is best just to let the thoughts flow. To hold them back and to give in to maladaptive thoughts such as, "it's hopeless," "there's no solution," and "I'm overwhelmed by this," prevents one from using his innate abilities to work through the situation. The seeker is asked to be still, to be quiet, and to allow his mind to wander and entertain solutions. After one opens the mind and allows ideas to come, once every idea is gathered, the prudent ideas are selected. Feedback, opinions of others, and assistance are welcome. As one allows his mind to fill with solutions and possibilities, it will be necessary to evaluate the revelations which appeared. One way it can be done is by reading literature about the situation and the solution one has chosen. Books which educate a person on ways of identifying, acknowledging, and addressing the traumatic event can be read. Means of bettering one's circumstance can be researched and evaluated. By utilizing all ones resources, the best solution is found. After finally selecting the best possible measures to take, the individual can then begin to take action. In selecting the very best course to follow, the process of visualization can be used.

Visualization is an entity which has both spiritual and psychological impact. It is used to help people to relax and calm their minds and bodies. Also, it can be used to allow one to attune to Spirit's idea of the life he is meant to live. Mentally, it is seeing what you want or have to do. Spiritually, it is to realize that to each, life brings an award of one's own visioning. Visualization makes use of the concept that thoughts become reality, that we are what we think we are. As a result, as a course of action is selected, the individual can visualize himself taking all of the steps indicated in that course of action. He can see himself in the midst of the situation with all the key persons with whom he has to interact. He can see the light, hear the sound, and smell the aromas involved. As he sees himself confronting the situation, he can visualize himself as being completely successful, doing everything right, and moving to a state of happiness and well-being. Once visualized, he can rehearse the scene with another person. They can role play and practice together. The act of visualizing assists the person in enabling him to successfully overcome depression, move out of darkness and prepare for the eventual victory.

The seeker has to remember that he is trying to find a new way of living and ideas which he had never thought of before will come to him. It is good. It is growth. It is the time to trust one's intuition. Both mentally and spiritually, the traveler is being guided into a new direction. Visualization is the conceived part of the old saying, "If you can conceive it, you can achieve it." It is important to have the concept of the journey being completed. Each step along the way is to be viewed as growth and evolution. The seeker must now take action, which is the achieved part of the statement. To do nothing is to languish in depression. Ambivalence and inertia results in a spiritual quagmire and deadens the soul. After the best course or courses have been selected, it is best to embark upon the quest. Like a medieval knight preparing to go off to fight a battle in some far-off land, the depressed individual engages in positive, purposeful actions which are designed to help him reach the vision that he has seen. The actions take many forms and are unique to each individual. However, they all have the quality of being constructive and revealing.

Sometimes, despite the vision of hope which has been received, the seeker still does not know what he or she is to do. There is an inner urge, however. which says it is time to move and grow. It is necessary to take a step, even in uncertainty. Once the decisive step has been taken, the steps which have been revealed in the visioning, even if only briefly glimpsed, will become made known.

As the mission becomes more fully understood, the individual can begin to set goals and make plans for himself as to what to do next. No matter what the task is, it is important not to underestimate it and to give it credence for it moves one forward. It is important to remember that no matter how grand and glorious the ultimate goal may be, it is possible to obtain. So, the individual begins the plan. If the goals are lofty, the seeker can think of making small steps along the way. With the successful completion of each goal, a greater sense of well-being takes place. In overcoming depression psychologically, it is important for the individual to realize that he has power, that he has the ability to change his life. To refuse to take action and to dwell in hopelessness continues the state of despair. Working on goals increases the sense of power and potency. Achieving the goal completely contradicts the person's image of himself as hopeless or helpless.

Spiritually, setting goals and working on them is much akin to accepting that faith without works counts for very little. Setting goals and working on them is putting one's faith to the test. Although God never tests us, we do test ourselves. God is with us always and forever and wants only the best for us. However, sometimes we fail to really believe that and at those moments it is necessary to go ahead and make an effort. In those moments we are to put our faith to work. Through the power of faith and the spirit, the goal will be achieved, and, if the goal is not achieved, then something better will. What is essential is to mobilize one's faith and move towards the light.

The purposeful action does not necessarily have to be for ourselves. There is a greater good which is achieved if one gives compassionate service to others. Selfless service is one of the highest forms of action, and as one gives it, not only is the ego diminished and psychological well-being increased, but spiritually one truly evolves.

In order to achieve the goals which we set, we may have to try new solutions and ways of doing things. The old methods may not work. In fact, often they will make matters worse. It has been said that in the darkest nights and in the greatness moments of trial, Spirit brings us insight and revelations which can guide us through the perceived darkness. Additionally, in our visioning, new solutions to the challenges we have are made manifest to us. Intuitively, we come to know the means to our ends, and so, we try to use techniques and new knowledge that we now have. The individual experiments and applies his answers to the challenges to see if he can meet his goals and move forward into greater awareness and well-being.

Initially, the understanding may be flawed. An experiment with a new solution may fail. However, it is no reason to lose heart. As the solutions are applied, they are refined. Through the refining, they are more able to meet the tests that the seeker has been given. It is through insight, revelation, and trial and error that a way will be found. The seeker is encouraged to remember during this time that he is never hopeless, but each insight and revelation brings more solutions and better enables him to overcome the seeming obstacles.

As has been mentioned, a real danger that surfaces when seekers feel sufficiently hopeless and worthless is that of suicide. The thoughts become, "What is the point of it all?" "There is no need to even continue to live." At those times, it is important for the seeker to remember his vision of journey's end and the good that awaits him when he reaches his destination. Also, the memory of the vision serves to counteract morose thoughts for the vision is grand, and the goals which come from it propels the person forward with a steadfast purposefulness. Again, the very act of doing something puts to a lie the maladaptive thought that the individual is helpless, and even the smallest success defeats the thought that life is hopeless. Every glimmer and every insight shows the seeker that there is indeed something to life and there is a promise that has yet to be fulfilled.

With insight and revelations the individual will be shown new ways of taking action. In cases of clinical depression when conventional therapies may seem to fail, the person will be shown another way. Alternative therapies will be recognized. Simple activities which influence well-being, such as exercise, will become appealing and the seeker may do something such as beginning a running program. Vitamins may be taken, which increases the person's physical health. Meditation as a discipline may be incorporated to move a person into a better state of being. The mind is kept open and is filled with solutions. The person has to determine and accept what he needs.

In deciding what is necessary for himself and in selecting his best solution, the seeker needs to ask himself some basic but very important questions. The first question to ask is, "What brings about the highest good?" The answer needs to reflect, not only the highest good for the individual, but the general good of all persons involved. As the pros and cons of the course of action are analyzed, the risk and benefits are weighed. The way which brings forth the highest good for all concerned is the way to go. One belief that is generally true is that, if a person determines something that is the best course of action for himself, then, usually, it is the best course of action for all persons involved.

The next question which must be answered is, "Is the solution harming anyone?" Although it may be benefiting the individual the question remains, "Is it doing damage to another person and denying them their good?" Ernest Holmes, the founder of the

Science of Mind, says an individual is entitled to all of the good in the universe he may desire so long as it does not take from the good of another. The best solution is in harmony with that fundamental principle. Adhering to the principles and honestly answering the questions concerning one's good aids in evaluating the best solution and selecting the most promising path to take. Each goal that is met is a step along the trail out of the wilderness. As the seeker begins to mobilize and make progress, many ideas and options will be revealed to him. His role is to be accepting. It is to be open, without judgment. The individual is to entertain every thought that passes through his mind. Nothing is to be rejected out of hand. As he applies his new-found knowledge, he is to be flexible. Rigidity and trying to make life be a certain way, especially the old way, will not work. One must be fluid like water or as flexible as a young sapling tree which bends this way and that to survive the mighty winds of a fierce storm. They are the inherent qualities which allow the individual to survive. As one's efforts become more successful, the downward spiral that was leading into deeper depths of despair is reversed. With each success, something new is learned. Something new is gained. The insights and wisdom which have been obtained and which are benefiting the individual are consolidated and become a part of his new foundation of self and understanding. Often the individual stops and begins to review his life. Sometimes it is not only the stage through which he has just journeyed but his entire life, the entire journey, and he begins to contemplate his very being.

It is only natural to look back on such a devastating and significant journey. In the reviewing, the person is changed. His knowledge is consolidated. The upward journey continues and is sometimes even accelerated. Success breeds more success. Understanding leads to deeper understanding. With new concepts of self, a new image emerges and a greater sense of well-being takes place. There is a glimmer of the dawn. The night seems to be breaking and the sun is just beyond the horizon. The soul which has been suffering now seeks to become established in what has been learned. The mere thought of what has been experienced can be terrifying, and there is no desire to undergo anything like it ever again. Strategies and plans by which to maintain well-being are examined and recorded on one's mental tablature. With new-found wisdom, the seeker may put into motion plans by which he maintains a healthy outlook and state of mind. A completely new lifestyle may emerge from the changes which have been made. Spiritually, a greater awareness of one's divine nature and a more satisfying spiritual practice may be obtained. All serve to keep the individual from re-entering the hell from which he just exited. The seeker is steadily evolving to higher levels of consciousness and well-being. There is no wish to turn back.

There are those, however, who despite their best efforts and intentions remain in deep depression. There is no movement. They are stagnant. St. John of the Cross describes these individuals as the ones who are inclined towards melancholy. He said, "They become greatly to be pitied since they are suffering so sadly. For this trial reaches such a point in certain persons when they have this evil humour."[1] The humour of which he speaks is what was thought of in medieval times to be a fluid or semi-fluid which was present in the human body, or even in the blood, which caused a person to have certain traits or a particular constitution.

There were four humours and they were thought to predispose a person to certain illnesses or disorders, one of which was profound depression. St. John of the Cross concluded that the "evil humours" or impurities attacked the soul through the medium of melancholy. The sufferers were only free when they were rid of the malevolent humours. Although the pain is intense when the soul enters the dark night, it is purified by the grace it encounters in the holy process and finds itself rid of impurities one after another and enters into a state of well-being.

It is interesting that it took centuries before modern psychiatry established the theories of biochemical processes which govern moods and account for depression. The medieval philosophers and scientists were even then aware that there were properties of the body which influenced depression. Persons who possessed a certain type of humour were thought to be frail, easily disturbed, and prone to melancholy. In modern terms, we know that there is a familial genetic predisposition towards depression. First degree relatives of people with depression have a higher incidence of major depression than the general population.

Modern research and psychopharmacology have identified the malevolent humours as being deficits or dysregulations in the neural transmitters serotonin and norepinephrine. The psychopharmacological theories have led to the development of a host of antidepressant medications. The medicines assist people who are melancholic or profoundly depressed in overcoming their depressive state when all other means seem to fail. Numerous psychiatric studies have shown that antidepressants work. Whether used alone or in combination with psychotherapy, the medications are effective. In fact, it has been accepted in psychiatric literature that without them certain types of depression never seem to improve. The medications in combination with psychotherapy tend to have a better outcome than either one alone. As a result, in overcoming depression, in moving through the dark night of the soul, medication can be a viable tool.

Many people describe themselves as naturalists or metaphysicians and because they are naturalists and metaphysicians may refuse to take medication. However, it astounds me that they will take herbs and teas by the handfuls and by the buckets. They will brew remedies, spend time, and expend energy to mix naturalistic ingredients but refuse to take pills which may only require a few seconds to ingest. They argument that medications are not natural and that they have side effects. Yes, the medications are processed. They are manufactured, that is true. However, as with all things, they ultimately come from nature. It is true that the medications have side effects. In fact, all medications have side effects, even the ones which are the most beneficial. Penicillin has side effects and can cause a very severe rash for people who are allergic to it. If a medication has side effects, it does not mean that if you take it you will suffer those symptoms. What is being described are things which can possibly happen. The probability is that they will not occur. The person simply needs to be informed of potential undesirable occurrences.

In point of fact, some side effects are desirable. People who are overcoming depression often cannot sleep. There are a number of antidepressants, many of them older medications, which have the side effect of sedation. When given at night, they are instrumental in helping a person to experience a good night's rest which aids in his recovery. A common myth is that because an herb or ingredient is natural it cannot harm you. It simply is not the truth. The great philosopher Socrates was executed by being forced to drink a cup of hemlock, a naturally occurring plant.

There are natural ingredients which are used to treat depression. Among the most famous natural remedies are St. John's Wort, ginkgo biloba, and valerian. St. John's Wort has the most data to support its usefulness as an antidepressant. At least one meta-analysis involving 23 randomized trials concluded that there is preliminary evidence supporting it as being superior to placebo in patients with mild to moderate clinical depression. On the other hand, at least one multi-centered, double-blind placebo controlled trial in the United States found no advantage to it over placebo. More recently, another trial from Europe concluded that it was superior to placebo. However, if one decides to use the herb, it is important to know that the plant is not innocuous. It is not a harmless item. Potentially, serious adverse affects can occur. Among them are gastro-intestinal symptoms, confusion, dizziness, fatigue, and sedation. Women who are of childbearing age and are at risk for an unwanted pregnancy need to know that it may compromise oral contraceptives. In addition, it can increase the clotting time for people who are on anti-coagulant medication.

Gingko biloba has been studied in Europe for the treatment of vascular dementia and has been reported in literature to have antidepressant activity. The studies are few and appear to be inconclusive. However, it is known to have several adverse side effects which include gastrointestinal disturbance, headaches, restlessness, and dermatitis.

Ginseng is cited as being effective for multiple symptoms, including depression. However, there are no controlled studies.

Valerian is a well known folk herb which has been utilized for centuries. Mostly, it is used as a sedative and a treatment for seizures. Although it is useful in inducing sleep, it has no known efficacy in depression. Also, it has a side effect of potential liver damage.

Modern pharmaceutical antidepressants were initially discovered serendipitously when the medicines were investigated to see if they would do other things. Researchers found that although the medicines did not resolve the condition for which they were intended, the recipients felt better. They were then investigated for their antidepressant properties. As researchers became more knowledgeable in terms of the things which caused antidepressants to work and to develop theories on the mechanisms, the knowledge was used to manufacture a whole host of new antidepressants. Nowadays, if someone is depressed, there are a number of medicines in several pharmaceutical classes which can be used to treat the ailment. With so many major treatments available, it is astounding that people will sometimes choose to be depressed. There are those who think they are supposed to be depressed because that is how it has always been. Others feel it is a stigma to take medication. Still others are ashamed of taking the medicines they need and view it as a sign of weakness.

Once, a woman wanted very much to talk to me. When I

met her, she was insistent on having a conversation and wanted to meet for lunch to continue to talk. I took her phone number, agreed to call her, and set a date to have lunch or a late breakfast together. When we met, she let me know why she was so adamant about speaking with me. She wanted to take advantage of my professional expertise. For years, she had suffered from depression. Finally, she was placed on an antidepressant, and it was effective for her. She felt much better and could continue her life in a much brighter frame of mind. Still, she was conflicted about her situation. I asked her what medicine she took. She said, "I take Prozac." I asked her how often did she take it, and she said, "I only take half a tablet every other day," which amounts to 10 mgs. of Prozac three or four times a week. Nonetheless, she felt weak and ashamed that she depended on taking the medicine for continued well-being. I asked her what happened when she did not take the medication. Her answer was that she would inevitably fall into a profound, miserable depression. I laughed and told her that if she can take half a tablet of a medicine every other day and stay well, then she needed to count her blessings. How wonderful it is that she knew what to do and that it took so little effort to remain in a state of well-being.

I further informed the woman that it was not weakness but simply wisdom to take what one needs. Her attitude is not unusual. I encourage anyone who finds that they have need of antidepressant medicine in order to overcome the darkness to take it. In my view, it is all here for a reason. I do not believe that Spirit labels all natural medicines good and all pharmaceutical medicines evil. They all come from nature and all medicines, whether herbal or pharmaceutical, have both beneficial and adverse effects. In using natural medicines, it is advisable to seek the counsel of a herbalist or naturopath, someone who has expertise. Pharmaceutical medications are to be used under the supervision of a qualified physician. Once a person knows what he needs, he can pretty much continue on his own with the assistance of the experts when necessary. Visits to the healthcare taker would become relatively infrequent.

To refuse to use an aid which would help one through the dark night is contrary to reason. It is best to leave stigmas and prejudices aside and to open one's mind. Who knows in what form his healing will take place. It is best to be open and receptive to it in whatever form it may come. If, for some reason, a person may need an antidepressant to overcome depression and move through the dark night of the soul, there are a number of medications which are available. If given an adequate trial and therapeutic dosages, they all work and are beneficial to most people. The original old line antidepressants, known as the tricyclics because of their biochemical configuration, are quite effective. They have the advantage of being long acting and being able to be given once daily usually at night because many of them have the side effect of sedation. As a result, they are an aid in inducing sleep.

Among the better known are Tofranil (Imipramine), and Elavil (Amitryptiline). The drawback with tricyclics is that they have major undesirable side effects. They can cause dry mouth, constipation, tremulousness, sexual dysfunction, and even urinary retention. Among the most dangerous side effects is that they can affect the heart and cause cardiac arrhythmia leading to cardiac arrest. However, it occurs in massive doses, and if the medicine is taken as prescribed, it is quite safe.

The monoamine oxidase inhibitors are another old line first generation class of antidepressants which are seldom used these days because of dietary restrictions when they are given and also because they can precipitate a hypertensive crisis if the dietary restrictions are violated. Nonetheless, the medicines are quite effective, and when used properly, can make a major difference in someone's life.

The first generation antidepressants have been in use since the 1950s, but are still used today, and in some cases may even be preferable to the more modern day medications.

The second generation of antidepressant medications began in the 1980s with such medications as Prozac. The newer medications are much less dangerous than the older ones. Also, they have fewer side effects. After being introduced, they quickly became the preferable first line of treatment. When used at an adequate dose over a sufficient period of time, they are able to alleviate depressive symptoms. They also are not without their side effects, some of which are paradoxical. For instance, the serotonin selective reuptake inhibitors (or SSRIs, as they are frequently called), of which Prozac is a prime example, can cause some people to feel sedated. On the other hand, it can affect others in such a way that they are hyper. Whenever I prescribe the SSRIs, I inform people of the paradoxical nature of the medicine and ask them to take their very first dose in the morning. If after taking it they feel sedated, that means that the SSRI is best taken in the evening for them, so that it may assist with sleep. In fact, taking it at bedtime would be the best time to take it. If, on the other hand, it causes them to be elevated or enlivened, they are to keep taking the medicine in the morning, so long as it does not make them anxious or hyperactive. As a result, they have more energy and are better able to function.

Among the side effects for serotonin selective reuptake inhibitors are hypersomnia, insomnia, gastrointestinal disturbances such as nausea and diarrhea, and dizziness. People who take the medicine also need to know that there is a significant incidence of sexual dysfunction. Although it does not happen to most people, it happens often enough to be of concern and an individual may want to try a different medicine if the side effect is sufficiently disagreeable to him.

The SSRIs commonly used today include Prozac, Paxil, Zoloft and Lexapro among others. Medicines of different biochemical class which are also used, particularly in today's pharmaceutical market, are Trazadone, which is often used as a sleep additive, Wellbutrin, and Effexor. There are other medicines which have not been mentioned and still others which are being developed.

There are a number of guidelines which are important in using antidepressant medication in returning to a feeling of well-being and recovering from the depths of depression. The first guideline is to have patience. The medicines are not a quick fix. In our world today, people want to take a pill and magically feel completely transformed the next minute. That is not the way it works. Depression has taken weeks, months; even years to become manifested and it takes time to resolve. Although the depression is in the humours of the blood as is described in medieval terms, or is in the dysregulation of the neural transmitters as is described in modern terms, adding an agent to purify the humours or to return the neurotransmitters to proper biological functioning does not result in an instant cure. The medicines take time to work. The balance is slowly restored. The humours are gradually cleansed. The neurotransmitters are slowly returned to a state of equilibrium and balance. The sufferer needs to know that the medicine will not begin to take effect until it has been taken regularly in an adequate therapeutic dose for two to six weeks. Sometimes it may take even longer, as long as eight to twelve weeks. Patience is not only a virtue, it is a necessity. While waiting for the medicines to take effect and for the humours to be purified, spiritual practices and diligent work in taking therapeutic actions to resolve depression are important.

Another guideline which is important in using medications is to be conscious of the dose which one is taking. Some people are very sensitive and need very little. Others need much more than normal individuals. Each person is unique and medications have to be individualized to suit the person who is taking them. A medicine that will work for one person may not do anything for another. It is important to pay attention on an intuitive level and to know whether something is actually happening in one's body and is actually having a desirable effect on his nature and on his own individual constitution.

Another consideration is the duration of treatment. People who suffer from major depression usually require regular treatment for at least nine months, preferably a year. A recommended guideline is that once treatment has been started, the individual take his medicine regularly for at least the prescribed period of time of nine months to a year. It means taking the medicine every day. A common mistake in taking medicine for depression is that once the person begins to feel better, he will decide that he does not need the medicine and will stop taking it. The results are predictable. Almost inevitably, the person will do well for a brief period of time and then will relapse back into another profound depression. If, as the Saint says, the depression is in the humours and is an impurity of the bodily fluids, or is a neurotransmitter dysregulation as is hypothesized in modern psychiatry, it is necessary to take the required treatment to remove the impurities or to put the neurotransmitters back in proper balance.

Although the individual is starting to feel better, it does not mean that the impurities have been removed from the humours, or that the neurotransmitters have been restored into a homeostasis. It simply means things are working and the person is going in the right direction. He is moving along his path of transformation and growth. It is best to take the medicines regularly for the prescribed time period of nine to twelve months. When the period ends, the individual comes off the medicine gradually, decreasing the dose by an agreed upon amount with the prescribing physician every week until the medicine is no longer being taken.

When a successful course of treatment has been completed, the good news is that fifty percent of individuals never need the treatment for major depression ever again. The not so good news is that fifty percent of the people relapse and require treatment at another time in their life. There is no way of knowing in which fifty percent a person will find himself. As a result, it is necessary to monitor one's well-being and to pay attention to symptoms which may be seen as a recurring depression. If for some reason a person has another severe episode of depression and plunges deeply into another night of darkness, one can learn from what has happened before and begin another treatment with medicines and therapies which have worked for him to bring him out of his despair.

Following another nine to twelve months of treatment, the person may once again gradually stop the medication and terminate whatever therapies in which he may be involved. Again, the medicine is gradually decreased until it is stopped. An example would be if one was on Paxil, a well known SSRI antidepressant. If the person was taking a dose of 20 mg regularly, he may begin by taking only 10 or 15 mg for a week and then dropping that dose to 5 or 10 mg for the next week and continue to diminish by 5 mg weekly until the medicine is no longer taken. Once again, when the treatment course is completed, it is hoped that the humours have been purified and that the neurotransmitters are once more in homeostasis and biological balance. Fifty percent of the people who complete a second course of treatment never require treatment again. However, there is still another fifty percent who do. From a psychiatric standpoint, if a person lapses into a third major depression, it is necessary for him to remain on antidepressants for the rest of his life to avoid relapses. It has been my experience that people who suffer from recurring major depressions inevitably relapse into a profound depressive state whenever they stop their medications.

If one finds it necessary to take medicines in order to traverse through a major depressive episode or to pass through the dark night of the soul, then the individual needs to do what is necessary. To say taking antidepressants is a sign of weakness is a statement coming from the ego. A person who is sick with a severe infection does not refuse antibiotics. His ego does not tell him, "I'm strong and I don't need to take these bacteria killing agents." He or she takes them. Perhaps it is a lesson in humility that a person is learning as he continues his journey forward which causes him to need to consent to taking medications.

Whatever the reason, there is a lesson to be learned every step of the way through the dark night. Everything that we are required to do is for a reason. All the tools which are presented to us are for our personal use and benefit. It is all here for our growth and transformation.

NOTE
1. St. John of the Cross, *Dark Night of the Soul*, Image Books, New York, NY, 1990, pg 49.

Chapter 6

CASE STUDY OF THE REJECTED WIFE

Account of a very depressed woman using a number of means by which to conquer her condition and circumstances.

One of the most interesting and demanding cases I had during my time in private practice was with a woman who was going through marital conflict with her husband. She was a middle-aged African-American female, 56 years of age, with three adult children from her first marriage. She was in her second marriage, which had lasted 13 years. She was a very bright, highly intelligent woman who was self-employed as an accountant, and had been very successful in her business having sustained herself in a profitable manner for 17 years. However, for more than a year, she had been significantly depressed and was no longer working.

Her husband had asked for a separation. When she was interviewed, she described her problem by saying, "I am under stress. I am just stressed out." As she spoke about the situation, it became apparent that her problems actually began before her husband told her he did not want her and demanded that they part.

Prior to him making his demand, she was already having difficulty with a situation involving her work. In a building where she rented office space, there was a substantial increase in the rent. As a result, she decided to move. One of her clients enticed her to move into the building where he was the proprietor. Seeking to have affordable rent, she took the offer and moved into the space. It proved to be a mistake. She was an attractive woman looking her age but being fit and trim, tall and slender.

She was approximately 5' 7" or 5' 8", weighing approximately135 pounds. She dressed very well. She had brown skin and long black hair.

Once she was in the client's building, the man took the opportunity to approach her sexually. She was not responsive, but he persisted. What had previously seemed to be a desirable situation became one of sexual harassment. Physically, he never touched her, but there appeared to be a constant barrage of comments which bothered her very much. It took a toll on her. She tried to endure the situation because she wanted to have an office space which was reasonable. Staying there, however, began to cost her in other ways.

Gradually, the harassment and comments eroded her self-esteem. She began to think less of herself and it affected her mood. As she began to feel badly about herself, her production at work diminished. Although the husband had not yet asked for a separation, the two were not getting along well at home. In fact, he stopped having sex with her, and the two had not had intimate involvement with each other for at least several months before she came to treatment.

When her situation crystallized and came to the fore, she became undone. The husband asked for the separation at least ten days before she came in for consultation. During that time, she was completely miserable. Not only could she no longer work, she was having extreme physical problems and somatic pains which caused her to have to visit her doctor. At one point, she even threw up blood. Her stomach was in agony. She could not sleep and was constantly tired. The depression that had been ongoing for at least a year and which had become in evidence for at least several months was now severe. By her own description, she said, "I can't work. I just want to die. Everything is an effort." By her own report, she said her personality had changed. She was usually very energetic and tried to do everything. Now she did not want to do anything except sleep. Although she was not suicidal, she even had a period where she had suicidal ideation and thought of driving off the freeway. It was brief, however, and she persisted in still wanting to live. She began to have some anxiety symptoms and actually suffered an asthma attack. She felt alien to her own self saying, "This is not me. This person that's going through all of this is someone else."

The person, who I will refer to as Mrs. M, was a clean living woman who had no drug problems and drank very little. There was also no previous psychiatric history. When she was first interviewed, she was very well groomed and immaculately dressed. She was very friendly in her manner and extremely cooperative. One would not have guessed, from simple appearance, that she was as depressed as she actually was. As she began to tell her story, however, she broke down into sobbing and was tearful throughout much of the interview. Her mood was one of pervasive depression. She spoke at length about how miserable she was, how her husband was rejecting her, how it caused her to feel terrible, and how it exacerbated depressive feelings which she already had.

As treatment began, the first thing that was examined was her medication. It appeared that the internist had given her an antidepressant which she had difficulty tolerating. It was Zoloft, one of the new generation antidepressants which are quite effective with many people. However, it can upset the stomach of some and evidently it was upsetting her stomach which has been described as being quite sensitive. An older generation antidepressant which promoted sleep and is known to be very kind to the stomach was chosen in its stead, that being Sinequan, which was to be taken once a day at nighttime only.

She then began to participate in therapy so that together we could determine how best to help her with her ordeal. In her personal history, she shared that she was raised in Los Angeles from the time she was six weeks of age. Her parents were together for 14 years of her life, but then divorced while she was a teenager. She described very loving relationships with both parents, but said she was especially close to her mother. She said of her father that she loved him, but they did not get along well and she was always verbally challenging him. She also had a somewhat conflicted relationship with her second husband who was asking for the separation. Although her relationships with her parents were generally good, she described her relationship with her siblings as only being okay. Mrs. M had one sister and two brothers; she is the youngest of the four siblings. She said that being the youngest and the smallest, they would pick on her and she would often have to run and tell her parents, so that her siblings would leave her alone.

Her first marriage took place when she was only 17 years old. Despite marrying so young, she was able to be in the marriage for 15 years. Her husband did not want her to work, but she was bright and wanted to make something of herself. She went to school and finished her bachelor's degree ultimately becoming a successful accountant. In the process of finishing school, she outgrew her husband, and the relationship ended. She had three children as a result of the union. At the time she entered into treatment their ages were: a son, 37; a daughter, 33; and a second son, age 31. The second marriage of 13 years bore no offspring, although the husband had a son of his own by a previous marriage.

In understanding Mrs. M's case, it became clear that there were a number of issues. Loss is the central theme of depression, and in her case, there were multiple losses. In addition, there were other factors which involved assertiveness and anger. Finally, the depression had become so severe that it was as Saint John of The Cross had described, "In the humours." There was now a biological component to the depression, and she required antidepressant medication.

In understanding the case, it appeared that Mrs. M had allowed herself to be subjected to ongoing verbal and sexual harassment for over a year. She took no steps to defend herself from it or to take an active stance against it. She bore the abuse and predictably it wore her down, eroded her self-esteem, and finally she succumbed to depression. Also, it appears that during that time she was in a marriage which had already shown itself to be troubled. She and her husband were not getting along. They were not being intimate with each other and had stopped being sexually active together for several months before he asked for the separation.

Additionally, there was the loss of her job and the income that it provided. Since she was so depressed, she could not work. She could not serve her clients as an accountant. She was very disappointed with herself. Her self-esteem was gone. Not only had she lost income from not being able to work, but the source of satisfaction which comes from having a successful business was lost. All that Mrs. M had lost culminated in one final loss when her husband decided that he did not want her. So, now there is the loss of the spouse and whatever love she thought he may have given her. It is no wonder that Mrs. M became extremely depressed. It is a wonder that she lasted as long as she did given what she was enduring.

Although it did not appear to me that she had entered into the dark night of the soul as there appeared, at least initially, to have been very little in the way of a spiritual component, it was quite clear that she was definitely in the shadow of depression. There were a number of steps Mrs. M had to take to overcome it. The steps were found to be beneficial to her. She was very open minded and motivated to become well.

Mrs. M had a number of strengths. She had an engaging personality which would win over many therapists, so that they would want to do all they could to help her become well. Besides being personable, she was also intelligent and resourceful. Her awareness of her depression was quite evident, so it was easy to engage her in the work necessary in therapy. Accepting how deep her depression was and the necessity for medication proved to be somewhat difficult. She had difficulty accepting the need for medicines and at first therapy was tried without it. One of the key moments in therapy was when Mrs. M finally accepted that she needed medication. It occurred after the Zoloft had been discontinued and the Sinequan had been started but also discontinued. Initially, she had difficulty with Sinequan because, despite being a medicine which supposedly allays stomach difficulties, it still bothered her stomach. It also caused her to be somewhat sedated in the morning when she awakened. Therapy was tried without medication. At first, she seemed to feel better, but then, she plunged into a deeper depression than she had experienced initially. Finally, a medicine was selected and an agreement was made to continue to work with it.

Two factors which are important in overcoming depression were the very keys in working with Mrs. M. The first of those was patience. She had a number of losses and a number of issues. As a result, it was clear that the case would not be simple and the treatment would take time. It was impressed upon Mrs. M that the contributing issues may take a while to resolve. She had no problem with acknowledging the need for taking time to treat her problems. She accepted it readily. She was prepared to be patient in order to bring forth a solution to all of her concerns.

The next step which was very evident in her case and is essential in overcoming many cases of depression was persistence. She would not abandon her treatment. If one medicine did not work, she would try another one. If one technique did not work, she would be open to another one. The doctor and the client together made many mistakes and sometimes took the appropriate step without knowing exactly why. It is all part of being persistent. There was a trust that was present during the treatment between client and doctor which allowed both to be persistent in the efforts necessary to resolve her situation. Patience and persistence served Mrs. M well as she battled through her own personal darkness.

Although she had many issues and losses, Mrs. M and I did not set them in a particular order. We both assumed that the primary issue was the loss of the marital relationship. One of the biggest problems was that, although the husband wanted a separation, he was not willing to leave the house. She was not working and could not afford to leave, so they were stuck there in the home looking at one another being angry and depressed. It was particularly debilitating to Mrs. M who said, "It is extremely depressing to me to come home and see him. I can't stand to know that he is rejecting me. It is hard to be with a man that I want but who doesn't want me." It caused her to break down into tears and would also precipitate somatic problems such as stomach distress and arthritic pains. Even with counseling and medication, it was hard for her to endure the situation of living in the same house with a man who wanted to be separated from her.

It was decided then that the first order of business would be for one of them to leave the martial situation physically. Either she or he had to move. She could not afford to move. She had no income except for disability which had been started and which I had continued for her by making medical reports on her behalf. She wanted to work but was simply too depressed to be able to do so. It took several sessions to boost her courage enough, but finally she was able to ask her husband to leave. At first, she simply could not accept the loss. Although he had not had sex or any type of intimacy with her for more than several months and had even told her he did not want her but wanted a separation, she still clung to the idea that he was her husband and they still had a relationship. It took time for her to really accept the fact that her marriage was over. After two months of discussing her adverse living situation, she was finally able to accept it, file for divorce, and put an end to the ambivalence. In accepting the situation and making a definitive decision, she began the process of healing.

Although Mrs. M did feel better, she continued to have significant depressive symptoms, and also, she had exacerbations of physical ailments and pains whenever she would have conflict or confrontations with her husband. Although she filed for divorce and asked her husband to leave, he still resisted leaving the situation and even asked her to go. Of course, she could not as she had no funds or income other than disability. In addition, he began to act angrily towards her because she had actually filed for the divorce. His tantrums and abusive words towards her further damaged her already fragile self-esteem. She continued to complain of how badly she felt because he had rejected her. She would react so violently to some of the statements he made to her and the angry behavior which he displayed that it would sometimes cause her to be so tense that she could not even eat. As he continued to display damaging behavior, such as taking some of her funds out of their bank account without her knowledge, she would have severe physical reactions to his treatment. On one occasion, Mrs. M was so ill she had to visit a local emergency room. She was experiencing persistent nausea, vomiting, dehydration, and weakness. Afterwards, she was even more depressed than before with diminished appetite and energy. It was clear something had to be done in order to restore her lost self-esteem and also help her to see that she would have to stand up to her husband and to the landlord who rented her the office space but then had sexually harassed her.

It is at this point that the psychological truth that she is a person deserving of good who is of equal worth to anyone else was stated. I did not mention anything about being a deserving child of God or anything of that nature as we had not explored any spiritual content up till then. She had given me no opening to insert spirituality. The spiritual truth that she is worthwhile and made in and out of the image of God is a spiritual truth which can restore self-esteem as one wanders through the darkness of depression.

We dwelled on the psychological principle that all persons are equal and she is as valuable and deserving as others. We dwelled on her being a good person who deserved to be treated decently. Soon thereafter, as if on cue, she spoke of an office visit which she had had with an internist whom she was seeing rather regularly because of her many somatic complaints. While visiting him in his office, he had hugged her and told her she was a good person. It was during a time when she was recovering from yet another of her many painful physical symptoms. She immediately felt good. The incident served to validate what she was being told. It helped her to know the truth about herself as a worthy human being despite the abusive derogatory statements her husband was making towards her. It was a significant moment which helped her to move further out of the wilderness towards the light. As her self-esteem increased, she began to have more strength to interact with her husband and actively planned to confront him to effect his departure from the marital home.

Another incident occurred when she took a trip to New York where she saw old friends. She had a good visit and was well received. It helped her spirit and boosted her self-esteem. When she returned home and faced her estranged spouse, she knew she could not go on letting him treat her the way that he had been. Up to that point, she had continued to cater to him, despite his ill treatment of her. Now, she decided that she would no longer defer to him or try to please him. All of her actions would reflect that she truly did want a separation. She was now willing to go ahead with it. After months of deliberation, Mrs. M's husband finally agreed with her on a specific date when he would move from the marital home. She was applauded for her efforts and for the progress she had made--although there was much further yet to go.

It was believed that the husband would move out of the house on the date they had set, but when it arrived, he did not move. In fact, a month after the date had passed; he was still living in there. Not surprisingly, the depression which seemed to be diminishing began to deepen. In session, her patterns concerning her husband were examined. Mrs. M was shown that she had a pattern of becoming more depressed and also experiencing physical, painful symptoms following conflict with or criticism from him. In order for the pain and depression to cease she had to find a better way of addressing the conflict. Despite increased self-esteem, and at least figuratively, accepting the loss of the marriage, Mrs. M still continued to be vulnerable in terms of her emotional reaction to her estranged husband. Mrs. M thought perhaps it would be helpful if she took more antidepressant medication, and she proceeded to do this which did help. She felt better. However, her energy and concentration remained poor, so she still could not return to work as an accountant. It was evident that her disordered thinking and patterns of dealing with her problems had to be further examined and changed. Finally, due to the divorce proceedings and the efforts of her attorney, the husband did move from the home. However, Mrs. M continued to have difficulty functioning, even without the stress of his confrontational presence.

A pattern began to emerge which Mrs. M, her internist and I could see. As a child, she had been criticized by her father with whom she often engaged in competitive arguments. Also, as the youngest and smallest of four siblings, she was often criticized and picked on by her older siblings. As a result, Mrs. M was vulnerable to criticism from childhood. It affected her in an adverse manner as she would not assert herself and relied on others to act on her behalf.

It was determined that whenever Mrs. M was criticized and brought into a conflictive situation, rather than dealing with it, she would internalize it. As a child, Mrs. M had developed the habit of turning her emotions within and running to her parents so that they might solve her problems for her. She would avoid directly confronting her older siblings or telling them how she felt. With her father, she simply argued with him, but then she suffered from his criticism. As an adult, the emotional energy of unresolved conflicts had to go somewhere, and since she could not express it in words or in actions, it found expression in her body. It manifested in the many upsets, pains and aches which she continually reported. An eye-opening experience happened with Mrs. M and her husband shortly after the observation was made.

Mrs. M and her husband met to discuss financial matters. He became enraged as they talked about their problems. He threatened her, and she picked up a knife in her defense. After the argument, she felt very ill. For the next week, she experienced weight loss, somatic pains, and difficulty functioning. She then recalled that as a child she would have an upset stomach whenever she was engaged in conflict with someone. She believed that it was related to suppressed anger. She had the insight after her pattern of ineffectual behavior had been pointed out to her. She made the association and gained critical insight about anger on her own. It proved to be very valuable. After that, Mrs. M began to give herself permission to express her anger verbally. She did not have to internalize it. She did not have to pick up a knife or make threats. She simply had to say, "I feel angry" in regard to whatever was the issue.

On one such occasion, Mrs. M spoke about how her husband was treating her in a mean way, and she was counseled simply to let him know that she did not like what he was doing and to tell him how angry she felt about it.. She did so. She did not try to engage him in resolving the conflict or seek some type of resolution to address her anger. She simply let him know how she felt about what he did. It proved to be enough to keep her from getting sick after the confrontation. It was a simple but effective change in behavior which probably saved Mrs. M many doctor visits and medical expenses thereafter. More importantly, it was a way of speaking and behaving that helped her to move further out from depression.

By this time, Mrs. M no longer mentioned the landlord who had been harassing her. In fact, she came up with her own solution to the problem. With the husband moving out of the house, she moved her office into it. She decided that henceforth she would simply run her tax accountant business from her own home. What a wonderful yet simple solution! By that, she rid herself of the harassing landlord and saved a substantial amount of money. She began to see the breaking dawn, which is the light shining at the end of the darkness. As Mrs. M. began to have success upon success, her depression began to lift. She continued to have periodic confrontations with the husband, but she handled them more effectively than she had previously. Fights over money continued to occur, and she, on one occasion, had to pay him some money as she had had his paycheck garnished because he would not give her spousal support; she paid him just to be rid of him.

In an effort to further strengthen Mrs. M, in one session the concept of self-control was entertained. The theme of the session was self-empowerment and determination. The whole point of the session was to let Mrs. M know that she, not her husband, had dominion over her life. It is a crucial point which people who are depressed have to understand. Often, they believe someone else has control of their life, and if the people would just do such and such, then everything would be okay. As it has been mentioned, it is simply false. By now, Mrs. M was aware that by internalizing her emotions she had not expressed how she felt to her husband and that had been the primary cause of her tremendous somatic pain. Now, it was further brought to her attention that not only could she refrain from accepting his abuse; he had no control over her. Mrs. M had the control. As a person responsible for her life and affairs, she was the one who decided what would happen in her life. She no longer had to give him power which he truly did not have anyway. Misguided statements based on misconceptions such as "he has control of me" ceased to be made by her. Not surprisingly, she began to feel better still. By now, she had moved beyond most of her depression and was rapidly leaving the darkness behind.

Mrs. M began to look for ways to be kind to herself in order to make herself feel better. When incidences of criticism or confrontation would occur with her spouse or even from her family, as she had older siblings who continued to mistreat her even to this day, she was able to deal with it. I took the opportunity to strengthen her self-esteem and concept of dominion over her life by saying that the people who criticized her had their own issues, and they probably had nothing to do with her. Also, she was reminded that she deserved to feel well and have people who cared about her. She began to become more active and wanted to deal with her final loss, which was the loss of her ability to work. By now, due to experiences and what she had learned from the time in treatment, she was beginning to set limits, be honest with herself, and express how she felt. The changes in behavior and in speaking caused her to feel much better about herself and, ,also, how she felt in general. She became even more active and eventually met someone, a middle-aged Caucasian male, perhaps one or two years younger than she, who appeared to like Mrs. M very much and whom she found physically attractive. They began to date, and he treated her very well. The relationship proved to be very beneficial to her continuing recovery.

By now, Mrs. M felt good most of the time. She did have moments of exacerbation of depression, usually centered on conflicts concerning money matters which she had with her husband. Although she was dealing with the situation satisfactorily, she wanted to feel better yet. By now in the sessions, we would discuss spiritual topics upon occasion. She began to attend a non-denominational inspirational spiritual center on a regular basis. She found comfort in it and began to incorporate prayer and spiritual affirmations into how she dealt with situations concerning her husband. Not only would she problem solve and engage in assertive acts such as limit setting or expressing her feelings, she also added prayer and spiritual affirmations where she affirmed the highest and best outcomes as manifesting in her life.

Continued pressure from her spouse concerning money and also from the insurance company which paid her disability began to cause Mrs. M to experience pressure to return to work.

By now, she had made substantial progress and a possible return to work was discussed. Before she felt ready to let go of the final loss of her job and was prepared reclaim it, she had a terrifying dream.

In one of the final sessions, Mrs. M reported having a dream where a giant snake was crushing her. In the dream, she was extremely fearful and thought she would die. The interpretation proved to be extremely fruitful. After making associations to the dream, it was found that the snake represented her fear. Fear was immobilizing her and restricting her actions. She was afraid of returning to work. It was her fear that was keeping her from returning. No longer was it an inability to work. Truly she had not been able to work for some time, but now she was ready. She had to cast aside her fear, stop restricting herself, and face the situation. She had to re-engage life and not let her fears crush it out of her. She resonated very well with the interpretation. She accepted it as being truth. Less than a month later, she had worked through her fear and was ready to return to work.

In the final session she said, "I feel good and I'm taking care of myself." Her disability was discontinued, and she was released to return to work and to pursue her career as an accountant. She had made it through the darkness and learned quite a bit about herself in the process. The case involved a long treatment, but it had a wonderful outcome, and Mrs. M made a number of changes in her thinking and acting along the way. She had insights about herself and put them into action to forge a better life. What she had learned about herself caused her to become stronger. Situations which had affected her, caused her to be ill, and depressed no longer had the power to do so in her life. Mrs. M did not lose heart. She was patient and persistent and worked through her challenges--qualities which are important to any spiritual or psychological progress. She dealt with several aspects of loss and was able to accept them and to recapture what she could. Finally, she was able to accept a rejection and let go of someone she had once loved. In exchange, she was able to reclaim herself and to reject abuse. Most importantly, she was able to dismiss anyone else having control of her life and to accept responsibility and dominion over it for her own self. Insights and reordered thinking based on seeing herself as a worthy individual, and also, one who is quite resourceful and able to stand up for herself were very important in her transformation back into a healthy individual. In the final analysis, Mrs. M was even able to touch the fringes of the dark night of the soul as she began to incorporate prayer and spiritual affirmations into her continuing recovery from depression and her ongoing journey into well being.

Chapter 7

Causes And Characteristics Of The Dark Night

The circumstances which lead to the Dark Night of the Soul, its spiritual essence, and its key differences from a depressive disorder.

Sadness and despair are common to both depression and the dark night of the soul. Both conditions have terrible moments of misery, periods where life does not seem worth living, and times when one earnestly wishes that he was dead. Depression and sorrow are strangers to no one. The fact that a person is extremely depressed does not mean that he has plunged into the dark night of the soul, although anyone who enters into the dark night will always experience depression.

Symptoms which are found in depression and also in the dark night of the soul are observable experiences, for example: insomnia, early morning awakening, intense crying spells, lack of energy or motivation to do anything, loss of appetite, and even loss of weight. There are other symptoms and conditions which can be mentioned as well. When a prevalent depressive mood and a cluster of symptoms are found in the same individual, the psychiatric association, by use of agreed diagnostic criteria, will diagnose the person as suffering from a condition known as major depression. When depression occurs, aggressive treatment, including intense psychotherapy and medication, is often indicated. Even so, despite the clinical severity of the depression, the person still may not be considered as walking through the dark night of the soul. A depressive disorder and the dark night of the soul differ in at least two very key areas. According to St. John of the Cross, there are two dark nights of the soul, and each night is associated with a period of purgation.

The first night is a time of sensual purging. The soul is cast into darkness in order to be rid of the pleasures and impurities of the senses. The first purgation is bitter and terrible to the senses of the spiritual seeker. The sufferings of the body, the emotions, and the senses are painful and nearly unbearable. If the individual successfully endures the first purgation, the soul is made ready for the next one, which is of a spiritual nature.

According to the Saint, in the second night of darkness, "The soul is purged and stripped according to the Spirit and subdued and made ready for the union, in love, with God."[1] The second night also has profound suffering. However, the pain is now to the spirit. Only a very select few enter into the second dark night of the soul because of it being of the Spirit. Physical elements have no power in the second dark night, and the sensual self cannot affect the process which is happening. Man, by his own might and effort, cannot pass through the second dark night. Only the most sincere, the most practiced, and the most proficient of spiritual seekers will transcend to the second dark night of the soul, and only then by their surrendering the sense of self and allowing the love of God to woo and guide them can they make it through the second night. Of themselves, they have no power to move through it. They must become passive passengers in the vehicle of God's love. It is important in their surrender that they have faith and believe that divine love is seeing them through, even when they do not perceive it. In a physical and emotional sense, they will be unable to perceive it for the love that is now passively carrying them along is of the divine nature.

Although the second dark night of the soul is an extremely rare experience which will be encountered by a precious few chosen individuals, the first night of purgation, the sensual night of the soul, is common to many. The time it usually occurs is when a person earnestly begins to travel along the spiritual path. He is in the beginning phases of truly practicing and living by spiritual truths and principles which he has found. The person is working hard to have higher consciousness and a deeper relationship with God. He may be working diligently at what he has discovered and even be filled with zeal. However, he is still a spiritual beginner. The dark night of the soul begins for him when, for God's own reasons, He chooses to draw the individual forth from the state of beginners who simply meditate on their spiritual road, and puts him on a path towards progressives who are contemplatives contemplating and practicing a deeper spiritual life, so that they may arrive at a state of perfection, more prepared for the divine union of the soul with God.

So then, the seeker enters into the dark night of the soul when Spirit calls him or her to move to the next level. Beginners on the spiritual path are to become contemplatives, to become seriously engaged in their spiritual practice. Rather than engaging in exercises to be a better person or to be more ethical or moral, they are asked to dedicate their lives to God. It is not an easy calling and many struggle and resist. They simply are not ready. Their motives and ambitions may not be pure. Saint John of The Cross said, "The path to eternal life is narrow" implying that the spiritual traveler must be unencumbered and detached from material things. The seeker must, in a sense, be removed from the sensual world. It can be interpreted as meaning that, in order to attain higher consciousness and merge into communion with the Infinite, one must divest himself of many impurities and destructive ways. The mind must be cleansed of sense mentality so that the spirit can take over it.

The purging of the individual soul, when he receives the call from Spirit and decides to heed it, is the true reason for the dark night of the soul. It is that which truly distinguishes it from a depressive disorder. In moving from a meditative state to one where he is a true contemplative and dedicated seeker on the spiritual path, the traveler is no longer seeking pleasure in spiritual pursuits, which can be delightful, but is seeking a deeper awareness of God. In fact, the spiritual activities which once brought so much joy no longer are found to be pleasing as the soul is yearning for something more. It is the time when certain characteristics of the dark night of the soul become manifest. When it happens, the seeker knows that there is a spiritual element, a profound one in fact, to his depression. He is truly walking in the darkness. Purging is about to take place. The only way to be rid of the intense yearning, sadness and despair is to go through the purification process.

The first trademark is that of melancholia. Many of us are familiar with a melancholic state. Almost all who has reached adulthood have felt it at one time or another. When a person is melancholic, he cannot perceive any happiness or joy. There is nothing that can make him feel good. Melancholia is characteristic of very deep depression, but it is also a trademark of the dark night of the soul. The reason is because what once caused a person to be filled with delight now brings him no joy whatsoever. There is no reason to smile. Most people consider it normal if it passes quickly. It cannot endure because if it does, it will make them so that they cannot function. Those who are experiencing major depression sometimes enter into the melancholic state on an extended basis. The person can become so ill he will not bathe or dress himself. He does not eat and, indeed, will likely starve unless forced to take food. Neither sex nor wine nor comedy nor any pleasures of the flesh can delight him.

In clinical psychiatry, these people are the ones who are referred to receive electro-convulsive therapy (ECT) also known as "shock therapy." It has been my experience that depressives who are so severe that they need ECT do benefit from the treatment and improve. They come out of the vegetative state and slowly begin to overcome their depression with the assistance of supportive therapy and services. One who is moving through the dark night experiences a similar melancholy and he is unable to receive pleasure, not only from conditions of the world, but conditions of the spirit as well. Indeed, the biologically-derived melancholia of the humours and that of the darkness look the same. Indeed, initial treatment may even be the same. However, there is something more to consider.

The second and perhaps most important characteristic of a person who is in the darkness of purification is grief over not serving God. The person feels as if he is backsliding. He does not feel as if he is completing his God-given mission on the planet, and has fallen short of the glory. There is an intense desire to serve God and a belief that he has not done so. The grief that is experienced is heartfelt and painful to the mind and to the body. However, although it may not be perceptible, the spirit within is becoming strong.

A third way by which the traveler is made known to be moving through the darkness of the soul is by the fact that there will be no joy in doing the spiritual exercises that he once did. The spiritual traveler may experience that the meditative practices and rituals which served him well in the beginning no longer work. As previously mentioned, not only does he receive no pleasure in the things of the world, but he fails to find joy in the representations of Spirit. The reason is because God is no longer communicating with His chosen one by means of artifacts or activities but will from henceforth communicate with him directly through contemplation. When lost in the confusion of the dark night of the soul, however, the spiritual seeker cannot perceive the truth. He mediates but finds no solace. He prays but feels lost and unheard. He does penance and spiritual works, but finds no comfort. In fact, all the work he does he thinks is displeasing to God, and he finds no favor in the divine sight.

In order to move through the purgation, it is necessary to be divested of attachments to certain rituals and objects which are associated with Spirit and are termed spiritual and instead allow the contemplative process to begin. As the initiate traverses along the spiritual path, transformation begins. The desires of the senses are suppressed and restrained. Worldly habits and ambitions are more controlled. The love for God is ignited and the primary desire is only to be closer to the Divine.

When the spiritual seeker reaches the point where his desire to be nearer to God is stronger than his passion for worldly treasures, a great upheaval begins in his life. In moving from a novice in spiritual practice to one who has dedicated his life to God, not only does there come about a severe purging of the soul and of the sensual sense, there also comes about a traumatic shift in one's personal life. More than once, I have heard people who have suddenly become serious about their spiritual growth say, "Everything is going wrong. My whole world is falling apart." They quote incidences such as, "My wife left me," or "I left my wife." They are having trouble on their job, and in some cases may have even been fired. In other scenarios, people choose to leave work which they suddenly find completely unsatisfying, despite the fact that it may pay them a wonderful wage. The circumstances in which they find themselves only lead to more depression and turmoil.

I recall a wonderful couple who looked to all appearances to be ideal. He was a mature, handsome African-American male, and she was a mature, beautiful African-American female. They looked to be in their mid-forties. When I first met them, I was impressed with how compatible they seemed to be. She became involved in training to be a practitioner of Religious Science. Those who have been through the process know it is a very serious undertaking and requires dedication, long hours of study, and persistent effort to complete the training. As she advanced in completing her practitioner training to become a spiritual counselor of the United Church of Religious Science, her marriage slowly disintegrated and ultimately the couple divorced. There are other stories similar to the one just told. After wrestling with the issues, sometimes the individual is joyful about the outcome. Many times, however, he is deeply depressed about what has happened. It is all part of the dark night of the soul. The person is being changed, transformed, and his life is changing as a result.

In the beginning, taking the actions which help one successfully move through a major depression and engaging in regular spiritual practices such as prayer and affirmations will move one along through the darkness. Eventually, a point is reached where no amount of human effort can move the person further along. It is then that the person surrenders to grace and opens his heart wide to receive whatever God is to give. The only action the person can take is to abide by the love that he has found within himself for God. As the love is ignited and becomes aflame, the spiritual seeker will be transformed by it. St. John of the Cross describes the process as putting a log into a fire. The log of wood gradually has its impurities burned away by being emerged in the fire until it is eventually transformed and itself takes on the fire's own properties. He suggests that the love for God within the soul begins to consume it and causes it to facilitate the burning away and casting off of any residual impurities, so that the soul of the seeker becomes akin to Spirit itself.

Misery and pain surely are going to accompany many of the spiritual purges. The night may be dark indeed. The seeker will find he has to let go of spiritual ego such as taking pride in one's knowledge of scripture and his perfection of practice. He will be humbled. As he becomes aware of the many faults which he has embraced for so long and which are being burned away in the fire of love, the seeker will feel separate from God and unworthy of God's love. At times, he will be unable to practice any spiritual practices. Even then, the love of God is transforming him and carrying him along through the shadow. The seeker is being prepared, although he cannot see it, to overcome depression and move into the next stage of evolution, for the eventual, ultimate spiritual realization of divine union with God in love.

NOTE
1. St. John of the Cross, Dark Night of the Soul, Image Books, New York, NY, 1990, Pg 61.

Chapter 8

OVERCOMING THE TRIALS OF THE SOUL AS IT JOURNEYS THROUGH THE WILDERNESS

Spiritual practices and spiritual principles which help one to move through the Dark Night of the Soul, facilitate growth and transformation, and aid the individual in enduring to the end.

Overcoming the dark night of the soul is no easy task. In fact, it is quite formidable and very challenging. It is life altering and can instill deadly turmoil in the mind and in the heart. It is eloquently described by David in the Bible as he speaks of his own suffering and time of shadow in the 42nd Psalm where he says, "My soul thirsts for God, for the Living God. Where shall I come and appear before God? My tears have been my meat day and night while they continually say unto me, Where is thy God?"[1]

Regardless of how one comes to it and no matter what the cause, there are certain qualities which can bring the seeker through the dark night of the soul. A certain attitude must be acquired so that one may transverse the dark night. Some, when they are troubled, may become busy, active, trying to avoid painful feelings by engaging in activity. Others may engage in intense spiritual kinds of practices thinking that will do the trick. Although it is helpful, no amount of practice can ensure illumination or save the individual from what he must confront and endure. Still, others become withdrawn and reclusive. The seclusion can lead to further depression and actually be counter-productive. The most important thing for the individual to do when he finds himself immersed in the dark night of the soul is to be quiet. St. John of the Cross describes the following discipline as that which is best to engage in to overcome the dark night of the soul. It consists of "allowing the soul to remain in peace and quietness, content with a peaceful and loving attentiveness towards God."[2]

By abiding in the proper attitude, eventually a love is kindled in the spirit of the seeker which burns away impurities of the soul, gives him passage through the dark night and draws him nearer to God. Although it is essential to acquire and practice the soul remaining at peace and quietness in order to move through the shadowy woods, there are practices which can assist in maintaining the proper attitude of peacefulness and quietude with proper attentiveness to God.

One practice is that of regular prayer. Prayer is universal and is practiced in all faiths and spiritual traditions. It is available to all seekers at all times, and it can see them through seemingly insurmountable odds. We all long for and need a conscious union with the Divine.

At no other time in our lives is it more important to move towards it than during the dark night of the soul. Prayer is a vehicle which moves us into a greater awareness of the divine union. When we pray, there is an invisible force in our communion with God. It weaves itself into our very being and commingles our thought with the thought of Spirit. It is like food to a starving soul. It gives one the strength to keep going. Resources are discovered which might never have otherwise been found. As we pray, it is best that we realize that we can never be separate from God. The Holy Spirit is no emperor in some far-flung empire distant from us who hears our petitions at his whim, but God is an indwelling presence that is with us always. He hears our every call and knows our every thought. As we pray, we do not have to petition. We simply need to know that, every word we speak and every request we make, God already knows before we speak it. So, we pray as Jesus did, giving thanks for the prayer being answered, even as it is uttered. It is written that he said, even as he called Lazarus forth from the grave, "Father, I thank Thee that Thou hast heard me and I know that Thou hearest me always."[3]

As we pray affirmatively, we know that it is the Father's good pleasure to give us the kingdom, and that as no earthly parent would deny his or her child any good thing, that unimaginably more our heavenly Father will give us all we need. We are comforted. We are uplifted. We are invigorated. Truths are revealed and we are ushered along our spiritual path.

Another very important spiritual principle and practice which facilitates the process of transformation and overcoming the dark night of the soul is that of meditation. In my own personal experience of meditating for over 30 years, I have found it to be wondrous. Even after decades of regular practice, I still find it to be mysterious as well. There is no predicting what will be released from the depths of the mind as one meditates or what changes one will be led to make as truth is revealed to him or her. Like prayer, meditation is found in all religions of the world. In some traditions, it may involve the constant repetition of a holy name, of a brief sacred verse or a scripture. There are many forms of meditation and all of them can lead to liberation of the soul.

Among the many forms of meditation is mantra meditation also known as Japa yoga, a Buddhist form of mindfulness meditation known as Zazen, candle gazing, and meditation on the breath. There are a number of other forms of meditations, including contemplating sacred verses or the names of God and even the names of saints and sages. Even chanting the names and qualities of God or performing Tai Chi can be considered meditation.

What is common to all meditation, regardless of the spiritual tradition, is that it is a fixed focus of awareness. The mind is centered on one thing. Ultimately, if it is to be a spiritual meditation, the focus of attention needs to be spiritual in nature for only that which is born of the spirit is spirit, and only that which is of the spirit can lead one into a deeper awareness of oneness with God. So, although mediation alone may not be able to bring one through the dark night if he is simply giving intensive effort in trying to will himself through the shadowy wilderness, it is still essential if one is going to complete his spiritual journey.

The late highly respected Swami Sivananda, a widely known sage of modern Indian, says of meditation, "Without the help of meditation, you cannot attain Knowledge of the Self. Without its aid, you cannot grow into the divine state."[4] It seems then that meditation, in whatever form it takes, is necessary for spiritual advancement. In yoga societies, Japa yoga or mantra meditation is considered to be the royal road to the attainment of enlightenment. Japa is a Sanskrit word which means repetition of the name of God. Focusing on and repeating one of the many names of God in Hinduism sets up a vibration which purifies the mind, purges the body and raises consciousness. No matter whether it is mantra meditation, Buddhist mediation, or another form, ultimately the mere act of meditating puts one into a communion with the Divine. As the process happens, one becomes quiet. It is in the silence that the purification begins. It is not by personal power or skill that change is effected, but it is only by allowing and being receptive to the love and grace of the Spirit. As a result of the comfort and revelations meditation can bring, spiritual aspirants going through the dark night of the soul may mediate on a daily basis and sometimes two or three times a day. Then, there is the extreme where the person is so bereft of joy and in such deep despair that there is no energy even to move or to try to meditate. Even there, one can simply close his eyes and contemplate the Divine. It is necessary to allow it to serve as one's meditation until he or she can do better. Even Siddhartha, who lived in India roughly 2,500 years ago and who became the Buddha, used meditation to evolve. There are many accounts of the turmoil which he was experiencing when he sat down under the Bodhi tree to find freedom from the troubles of the world. It is said that he made a vow when he sat there that he would not arise from that spot until he was enlightened and if he did not find enlightenment, surely he would die. Death was preferable to the state of misery in which he lived at that time. Some say he endured a terrible night of pain and when he awakened in the morning after coming near to death, he arose an illumined being. Others say that the night of suffering is actually figurative, that, in fact, he sat on the banks of the Nairanjana River under the Bodhi tree for years before he became enlightened. Be that as it may, what is important is that a meditative state was essential for his transformation. Even the great Buddha mediated to go through his night of trial and tribulation, and when he arose he was no longer experiencing ignorance and darkness, but he was awake and aware. We can all learn from the "Awakened One" and use meditation to help us through our own personal nights and moments of shadow.

Regular meditative practice helps the spiritual aspirant to move along his personal path and is especially helpful when moving through the dark night of the soul. There is yet another spiritual practice which facilitates the process of transformation and purification. It is that of communion and fellowship with beings of like mind and aspirations. In the East, it is known as Satsang. It is a Sanskrit word which is sometimes spelled as Satsanga. Regardless of how it is written or pronounced, it means the company of the good and it refers to associating with the wise, the saints, the yogis, and the high-minded beings.

Satsang is vital to a spiritual aspirant. It is referred to in the Bible and in modern books on personal development. When one is in the dark depths of despair, Satsang has the power to bring him through it. The source of the power of Satsang is described in the New Testament in Matthew 18:20 where it says, "For where two or three are gathered together in my name, there am I in the midst of them." Here, it is made plain that when people are gathered together in acknowledgment of the Christ Presence, that which brought them together is right there with them. The Christ Presence, the Buddha Mind, the Krishna Consciousness springs forth and blesses all who are gathered there. Many of us have been uplifted when we went to be with others who came together in the consciousness of worshipping God. We may have entered the halls with our eyes downcast, our backs bent, and our souls at an ebb but left with our heads raised, our shoulders thrown back, and walking with an energetic stride for the Christ Presence had been touched and we had been brought to a higher place.

Modern authors also refer to the benefit of Satsang. Ram Dass, in his book <u>A Journey of Awakening</u> says of it, "A beginner in spiritual life is like a young tree that needs to be circled with a fence for protection."[5] It is the seeker's need for Satsang, a group of fellow aspirants who strengthen one another's sometimes shaky faith on the journey. It is good to regularly seek the company of the wise and the good as one journeys through the shadow. Indeed, there are those among the swamis and wise sages of India who thought that the practice of Satsang was one of the highest means by which an aspirant could reach God. One of the things that being in Satsang does is that it destroys isolation. People who are depressed and stuck in their own turmoil tend to isolate themselves from others. They feel worthless and alone, separate from God and humanity. To be in Satsang is to dispel those feelings and false notions and to bring forth the truth. As one enjoys the company of the righteous and the good, then it begins to dawn on him the knowledge of his own true nature and his relationship to the Divine. Yearning and devotion for the Lord becomes stronger. As the aspirant devotes himself to God, God devotes himself to the aspirant and draws him near to Him. Engaging in Satsang regularly is a very powerful practice for spiritual advancement and overcoming the throes of depression. It may be as simple as sitting with a prayer partner, singing holy chants with a group, or attending a church service. However one chooses to engage in association with the wise and the good, the benefits are assured.

There is yet other practices which aid the spiritual seeker as he moves along the path through the wilderness. They are those of engaging in good thoughts and the reading of spiritual and inspirational literature. Science of Mind, the Bible, psychology and even traditional Hinduism all agree on the powerful effects of uplifting thoughts and readings. Swami Sivananda, in his book <u>Sure Ways for Success in Life and God Realization</u>, says that if you read the writings of a saint, you are essentially receiving the same benefit as Satsang from that saint. If you study the writings of a great soul, it is the same as experiencing Satsang from that great soul. So then, if one cannot be with the Dali Lama or Mother Theresa, he can read their writings and be benefited almost as if he or she was in their presence. So, we can see the value of reading high-minded literature.

In modern Cognitive Behavioral Therapy, good thought or rational thinking is highly praised as being a tool by which one overcomes depression. Irrational thought which brings forth dysphoric feelings and maladaptive behavior is discarded and replaced by thoughts which are functional and encourage good behavior, thus helping one to move through depression. In the Bible, it is written in Matthew 7:17, "Even so, every good tree bringeth forth good fruit, but a corrupt tree bringeth forth evil fruit." Here, Christ is referring to our thoughts and our actions which, if they are good in nature, bring forth good deeds and good results, but if they are of "malicious intent," produce grief and destruction. Ernst Holmes, in the book <u>Science of Mind</u> further elaborates by referring to Jesus' statement that a house divided against itself cannot stand saying that only one's thought can overcome destructive thought, but so-called evil cannot eradicate evil. "The thought of good must ever overcome any thought that is less than good."[6] It all means that good thought can lift us out of the doldrums and deception. It means that the study of spiritual writings and uplifting literature can elevate our condition.

So, it follows then that in overcoming the dark night of the soul, the spiritual seeker is benefited by reading inspirational literature and engaging in right thinking on a regular basis. One's thoughts need to be rational. They need to serve a useful purpose. Psychologists might call it positive thinking. Spiritualists would call it good thought. It is all the same and it produces good fruit. One must be like the guards at the city gates who are mentioned in the Old Testament. They stand and watch all who enter in and all who depart through the city's portals. In like manner, the aspirant must watch his thoughts and dismiss those which serve him not, for they bear ill fruit and choose instead to dwell on those which inspire him and lead to beneficial service.

In a similar manner, reading and studying the inspirational words of the wise would guide him through his troubled times. Music also helps. Who among us have not been inspired by the heart-rending rendition of a sacred hymn? Gospel music, sacred chants, and other religious or spiritual music can help to heal the soul and cause the spirit to soar.

A very important tool to be used in traversing through the darkness is the spiritual practice of using affirmations. To affirm something is to claim that it is true, regardless of any evidence or conditions that would say otherwise. To continually affirm something is to cause the mind to accept something into consciousness that it wishes to believe. In its essence, an affirmation is a positive declaration. In the midst of depression and spiritual turmoil, an affirmation can be used to see pass appearances and to declare the truth. As a result, one can readily see how it would serve to assist him in moving through the stressful times and help him to progress further along his spiritual path. For an affirmation to be effective, it should be short and simple. Also, it needs to be done in the present tense. The seeker needs to know that the truth he is affirming is happening to him and is with him now, not in some far-flung future but in the present here and now.

Also, it is important that the person believes what he is affirming. If he does not, the affirmation cannot work. Also, it is best that the affirmation be stated in a positive way. One wants to move forward and upward, and not entertain negative statements. A simple affirmation that focuses on a spiritual truth can serve as a guiding light through the deepest darkness. The aspirant needs to repeat the affirmation every time he feels like he is going off track. He or she may repeat it many times during the day. It will serve to clear his mind and wash away false thinking and delusions.

One of my favorite affirmations is one which was told to me jokingly by the late Reverend Maurice McCracken, an elderly pacifist minister who had once been a leading minister in the Presbyterian denomination in Cincinnati, Ohio. The affirmation was simply: "This too shall pass." He would always say to me, "Herman, no matter what the trouble was, the scriptures said it came to pass. Thank God it did not come to stay." Indeed, we all need to be grateful that when challenges come, they do not remain. Eventually, they come to an end. The affirmation, "This too shall pass," serves as a reminder that although our plight might seem as if it is eternal, it has a finite ending, and if we can but endure, we will survive it. The simple saying has helped many a person move on through depression and even through the dark night.

Other examples of affirmations which have helped others to stay focused in overcoming their tribulations are statements such as the following:

1) "I am open to discovering new meaning in my life." The implication is that one is opening up his consciousness to come into a deeper understanding of his purpose.

2) "I believe that I can change and I am willing to change and grow." Change and transformation are a necessary part of overcoming depression and spiritual distress. The affirmation demonstrates a willingness which will help the aspirant with the transformations he has to make.

Examples of other affirmations which can be used to help a person through depression or spiritual unrest are "Every day

I'm getting better and better," "I have everything I need," and "God will see me through." They are all simple, but repeated constantly and given focus and attention with any degree of conviction, they will uplift and strengthen the seeker and bring peace to his mind.

An affirmation can be created which treats a particular thought disorder or condition. If one is feeling separate and alone, and apart from all beings, even God, there are affirmations which can be used to dissolve that type of thinking and debilitating emotion. An example of it would be something such as "I am not alone for a Presence goes with me and daily accompanies me wherever I go." A simple one which is very effective is, "God is with me always." Another affirmation which can be used if one is feeling deeply depressed is, "I cannot be sad or depressed but I am happy and glad for the All Good has claimed me as Its own." Constant repetition of an affirmation of its nature can instill joy in the soul.

Affirmations can be used to dispel doubt and give the depressed person or the spiritual seeker a feeling of success in his journey such as the one stating "I draw my Good to me and nothing can keep it from me." Another one is, "I am surrounded by the love of God and all is well." There are as many affirmations as the mind can imagine. If they are based in truth and spoken in the here and now with conviction and feeling, they all have the power to help in the transformation and movement of the depressed individual and the spiritual aspirant.

Another spiritual practice which is based on the omniscience of God and His Presence in all beings is that of intuition. Intuition cannot be forced and cannot be regularly practiced on any basis for it comes in and of its own self. It is the God in man revealing to him the Truth of his being. Intuition places man in direct contact with Ultimate Reality. During the dark night of the soul, insights and revelation will come to the spiritual seeker. Even in his bleakest moments, and perhaps probably in the bleakest of moments, there will come to him a flash of light. It is the illumination given him by intuition. The gift of intuition is to give the aspirant the tools he will need to further move along his path of purification. The task of the spiritual seeker is to always be available to spiritual illumination.

In the throes of despair, the mind may shut down. The spirit may be in such turmoil that it cannot recognize when it is being given a gift which will lead it into the light. Even at his darkest moments, the spiritual aspirant needs to maintain the awareness that intuition is always with him, for God is always with him, and understand that at any moment divine knowledge may make itself known to him. There will be moments of "ah ha" and epiphanies when least expected for God truly wants the seeker to complete his journey. God does not want to leave him in darkness. Maintaining the consciousness that intuition is always with him and being prepared to recognize Truth when it comes to him is very important for the aspirant to move through the shadow into the light.

Two more important practices in moving through the wilderness are visioning and visualization. It has been said that if one can visualize a thing, then he can do it. To visualize a performance often leads a person to complete the performance in life. Psychologists often use the process of visualization to help people learn new skills in behavioral therapy. It is useful in overcoming anxiety, but it can also be used to assist with conquering depression. Mentally, we see what we wish to have or complete, and in so doing our minds accept it as a reality, or at least a possible reality. It empowers a depressed person to be able to visualize a happy life. It gives strength to the spiritual aspirant to visualize the end of his journey and to see himself as moving into divine union with God.

Although visualization may be sufficient for someone who is overcoming depression, it may not be enough for the person who is moving through the dark night of the soul. One may have to move beyond visualization and into visioning. Because of the fact that when we visualize things we are actively using our own imagination to create images, visualization is necessarily limited. Although we may imagine an abundance of joy and goodness, we are limited by our imagination which means moving through the shadow will require something more. It needs an opening up to God. An influx of the Divine is necessary. It is done by moving into visioning. We cannot know the new creature we will be when we complete our journey through the darkness. It may be far beyond anything we could possibly ever imagine. It will be God's idea of the new us. So, it is in visioning that we simply open up ourselves consciously to create a space where we are receptive to the spiritual ideal of us. As we become a conduit through which we allow the mind of God to operate, we are transformed and become what God wants us to be.

As we travel along our path in life, none of us know the form our help will take in times of trouble. Some of us think it will come in a certain way and only from select individuals. In so doing, we limit the resources which are available to us and may prevent ourselves from receiving services which are much needed.

There is an often heard old story that has many versions which speaks of people who carry a narrow view. A great storm was coming and was scheduled to hit a small town which was located on the banks of a river. All the weather reports said that the storm would be fierce and would bring lots of rain causing the waters of the river to rise. A man lived there in the town who had a comfortable home and was quite satisfied with his life. He listened to the warnings but paid very little attention to them. As the rains became heavier, the waters in the river around the town began to rise. One day, one of his neighbors came by in a big truck and knocked on his door. When the man answered, the neighbor said, "My friend, the waters are rising. Soon the town will be flooded. I have a big truck which can take us out of town. Your car may not be able to do it. Why don't you pack your things and come with me in my truck and you'll be safe."

The man thanked his friend and said, "I appreciate your offer, but God will take care of me. Thank you. Good-bye." The rains continued to fall and the waters continued to rise. Finally, the water was so high that the man had to move from the bottom level of his home to the top floors. While he was up there, a small group rowed by in a big boat. They called to the man and said, "Neighbor, the water is rising, the river is flooding. We think you might drown if you stay here. Why don't you come with us in our boat, and you will be safe." The man called back and said, "Thank you, neighbors. I appreciate what you want to do, but I know that God will take care of me," and the people rowed away. The rains continued, and finally, the water rose so high that the man could no longer stay, not even in the top floor of his house, and he had to go up to the roof. While on the roof, a helicopter's pilot spotted him, flew over to him and lowered a ladder saying, "Grab my ladder and climb up. The waters are rising. If you stay here, you may drown. Come with us, and you'll be safe." The man shouted back to the pilot, "No, thank you. I appreciate your offer, but I'm going to stay right here. I know that God will take care of me." Finally, the waters rose so high that the man could no longer safely stay on his roof. The current swept the man off the roof and into the river where he drowned. His spirit went on into the afterlife where he met God. When he did, the man said, "Lord, I prayed to you constantly, and I asked you to take care of me, but when the rains came and the river rose, the waters flooded my house, and I drowned. Why didn't you take care of me?" God replied to the man, "Didn't I send your neighbor to pick you up in his truck? Then, I sent a boat of people to take you out of the water. Didn't I send a helicopter to pick you up from the roof of your house? My son, you need not have drowned."

How many of us are like the man in the story? We want things to happen according to our expectations. Perhaps, he expected God to send angels down from on high which would carry him to safety or cause the flood waters to recede. The point of the story is that our help and our salvation can come from any quarter, expected or unexpected. Our task is to be open and available to the help when it comes in whatever form it comes. We are to accept it with open and willing hearts. It is all there to help us through our dilemma. God gives us everything we need to achieve our final victory over depression and over spiritual despair. We have but to realize it and be available to recognizing the answers to our problems when they arrive. The solutions may not be melodramatic and extraordinary, but they may be plain and very simple. They can come through the comforting word of a friend or a family member. Support groups, although they may not be Satsang, usually have a common purpose of self-help. Who knows who may be in the group and how he or she will affect you? If the mind and heart are open, there may be comfort and consciousness-raising activity to be had. Prayer groups, study groups, and prayer partners are all venues through which help may come.

Once as a young man, while still finishing my residency in psychiatry, I was undergoing a depressive phase. On a particular day, I was not working, but had no interest in the outside world electing to spend the time alone isolated in my apartment. A rather ordinary and totally unexpected event happened that brought me out of my depression and back into well-being. In my apartment complex, there was a tom cat named Melvin whom we all called the "community cat." For some reason, I had left my door ajar, and on this day, Melvin elected to visit me. He came in and looked at me before deciding to rub his body against my leg. He must have decided to stay awhile because he curled up in a corner of my small apartment close to me. There was something about his presence and his visit because I immediately felt uplifted. Somehow, the cat helped me reconnect with myself and, through him, all other beings. It could not have been a more ordinary and common occurrence, as it was a common ordinary house cat that was sent to raise my spirit. It is important to know that as we move through depression and darkness, help is always available to any who would but recognize and receive it.

NOTE

1. Psalms 42:2-3
2. St John of the Cross, *Dark Night of the Soul,* Image Books, New York, NY, 1990, pg 71.
3. John 11:41-42
4. Sri Swami Sivananda, *Sure Ways for Success in Life and God Realization,* The Divine Life Society, U.P., Himalayas, India, 1970, pg 1.
5. Ram Dass, *Journey of Awakening,* Banton books, New York, NY, 1978, pg 39.
6. Ernest Holmes, *The Science of Mind*, Penguin Putnam, Inc. New York, NY, 1938, pg 448.

Chapter 9

Spiritual Qualities And Reverential Activities In Moving Towards The Light

Various attributes and important attitudes as well as acts and rituals which are instrumental in staying on the path and completing the journey of purgation.

When a person is going through depression, he may often experience thoughts such as, "What's the use? I may as well give up!" There may be times when he is suicidal and contemplate taking his own life. While in the deepest depths of his night, the spiritual aspirant may want to abandon his path thinking that the goal that he seeks is impossible. There are spiritual qualities ingrained in all of us which are essential and need come to the forefront during the trying times and tribulations. The qualities engender hope when one would be hopeless, courage when one is discouraged, and the strength to continue. There are many, but the following spiritual qualities I think are probably the most important. It serves us all well to be aware of them and to use them as we continue along our journey.

<u>Patience</u>. Perhaps the most overlooked and important spiritual quality which is needed to move into the light is that of patience. In most all spiritual traditions, patience is considered a virtue which is desirable to be cultivated if one does not already have it as part of his character. In fact, it is considered to be vital if one is to overcome depression or have transformation of the spirit. The sages and saints of the East agree that without patience there can be no success either in the material or the spiritual world for we know that the aspirant will encounter difficulties. There will be obstacles along the way which will cause him to

want to abandon his quest. The difficulties, however, can be overcome with patient consistent effort. The aspirant is not to give up and throw away all of the benefits and insights achieved as he works hard to be elevated in consciousness. The aspirant is to call upon patience, place it the forefront of his awareness, and embody it for it allows him to endure all that he must in order to achieve his goal.

All of the great saints and all of the great sages of the world have had to have patience. They have had to endure pain and difficulties either to have their own selves transformed or to bring forth enlightenment to others. The seeker humbly submits to the process and, in so doing, commits to being changed and to enduring until the end.

<u>Perseverance</u>. Just as important as patience is the God quality of perseverance. Patience is that aspect of our being which allows us to wait with calmness and humility in anticipation that our change will come. Persistence is the quality which allows us to engage in consistent effort and action in reaching our goals-- even as we endure. In his book, *Dark Night of the Soul*, St. John of the Cross stated that even though the aspirant may feel as if he is doing nothing and is stalled along his spiritual path, it is quite sufficient if he has patience and perseveres in prayer. In persevering, he is aligning himself with a loving attentiveness to God. He keeps his eyes on his goal. His vision is single. He moves towards the light. As he maintains his vigilance, God will awaken within him, at some point, a spark of love and depression will be overcome by joy. However, if one is not persistent and gives up when the obstacles come, he will never know the joy or awaken to the awareness of a growing union with the Divine. The afflicted is to persist and embody perseverance, even as Job did in his suffering. For as surely as he moves towards a new dawn, all of the pain and suffering will come to an end.

<u>Trust</u>. Ernest Holmes, the founder of Religious Science, wrote in his book *The Science of Mind*, that learning to trust will make us happy. The implication is that to trust the universe is to

place oneself in right relationship with it and with the Divine Intelligence which rules it. It can then be affirmed that trust is a spiritual quality and is a sufficient, if not necessary, condition for feeling good. A person who is going through the dark night of the soul may mistrust his surroundings, the people he knows, himself, and even God. He is suspicious of nature and afraid of the universe. He is torn apart by confusion. The aspirant must begin to trust which also enables him to begin to dispel confusion. It is like sunlight which evaporates a lingering fog. One has to give in to his intuition and hold fast to it because it tells him that God is always God. It is necessary in the times of confusion and fear to know that no matter what conflict or turmoil we are going through, there is something which will carry us through the storm. It is imperative to believe that the Presence is there with us always thus allowing us to trust and to move into right relationship with God. Trust affirms reliance, not only upon oneself, but with the eternal Spirit. When we are afraid of the natural world and the spiritual realm both, we live in terror and suspicion. It is then that we are really living in darkness and are uncertain of the salvation of our own souls. Truly there is no time that has a greater need for trust. St. John of the Cross says for those going through the dark "Let them trust in God who abandons not those that seek him with a simple and right heart and will not fail to give them what is needful for the road."[1]

Discipline. Although it is necessary for spiritual practice, some will question as to whether discipline is truly a spiritual quality. I believe that it is. I am not speaking of the type of discipline such as a drill sergeant will use with a new recruit in a Marine or Army camp, nor am I thinking of the type of discipline that is required to go through extreme austerity which could be tortuous to the mind and to the body. Instead, I am speaking of the type of discipline which is the partner to perseverance and serves to keep the aspirant regular and in balance when all of his senses say, "Indulge yourself or give in to the weakness and to the fatigue of the journey." Spiritual discipline is more of a gentle urging which motivates one to move on rather than a tyrant which exacts a terrible toll if one does not do exactly as he says. In truth, a forcible discipline can be counterproductive to someone who is on a spiritual path when it is time to surrender to the will of the Supreme.

When I was in medical school on my surgical rotation, I remember hearing of a very successful, well established surgeon who was undergoing a terrible divorce. He had to leave the home which he shared with his embittered wife of many years and all of his financial assets; his other affairs were in turmoil. His colleagues knew the toll his divorce proceedings were taking on him, but he did not miss one scheduled surgery. He made all of his rounds and gave careful attention to all of his patients. When asked how he managed to do everything so well, he simply said, "Discipline." During his intensive training as a surgical resident, he had learned what is called "surgical discipline." It is the ability to concentrate and shut out all else and attend to the matter at hand, regardless of whatever else is going on around you. It is being there on time and prepared. The spiritual aspirant who is traveling along on his way needs to have such a discipline in order not to stray from his path. It is the decision to rise and meditate, rather than to lay there and languish in self-deprecation and despair. It is the urging and the desire to do what is necessary even when the senses say otherwise and there is an aching in the bones and pain in the heart. A gentle urging from within speaks to the aspirant telling him to wake up and rise like the sun does every day and engage in spiritual practices of prayer, meditation, Satsang and other activities which help him along the spiritual road.

Discipline is aligned with the laws of the universe. The laws of nature are regular and consistent as they always work. The law of gravity is a constant that always operates. The apple which leaves the tree always falls to the ground. Discipline helps us to be regular and steadfast in our spiritual practice, just as the laws of nature are regular and constant in their operations. Discipline even helps the spiritual quality of perseverance. In order to move through the darkness, the aspirant needs to be disciplined in his spiritual practice, withdrawing from the dictations of the senses, and focusing on the invitation of the Spirit. When the senses say, "lay still and give up," when the body is in severe agony, and the heart is failing, it is the time when one wants to become undisciplined. Despite all appearances, it is in periods such as these that it is time for discipline. It is not being harsh to oneself but coming forth with a gentle regularity, with a nudge away from the tyranny of the worldly senses and a step in the direction towards the Invisible. It is time to become a regular spiritual practitioner when the body and the mind cry for the soul to give up the journey. Even a limited discipline will lead to sufficient practice to overcome the laziness and the lethargy which would serve as a blockade to further progress. Let the aspirant exercise discipline, not in a harsh way, but firmly and regularly as he moves along his path through the darkness towards a new day.

<u>Faith.</u> The quality of faith is absolutely necessary for any spiritual progress or spiritual works. It is no less important in moving through the dark night of the soul. It is a quality which is often described and alluded to in both the Science of Mind and the Bible. Faith is the key to every religious tradition and to every transformation. Without our faith, there cannot be perseverance and there cannot be patience. In Religious Science, faith is described as a mental attitude and the belief in the presence of an invisible principle and law which directly and specifically responds to us. It is also known as the substance of things hoped for, the evidence of things not seen. Actually, the divine quality of faith is all of these elements and much more. It is a power through which we connect to the infinite. We touch the hem of the garment of the living God and all of His grace, power, and goodness become available to us. Faith is not a passive belief, but an affirmative and positive action.

If one truly believes and has faith, there is no doubt that he will endure and pass through the valley of shadow, not only intact, but stronger and more pure than ever before. To have faith, the spiritual aspirant has to reach onto the affirmative side of life, accept that God or Absolute Life is, and know that Infinite Power dwells in his innermost being. One also has to know and affirm that Infinite Intelligence and Infinite Power are on his side. When one knows that God, the universe, is for him and not against him, one has faith. People who have the quality of faith, however, are doers. They are not sitting passively expecting things to happen because they believe. They walk in the direction of their belief thus showing their faith. If they do not use their faith, then they have it not. The faith that one has is used to go through the turmoil of the dark night. It is during terrible times that one remembers the promise of the living God when He said in Hebrews 13:5, "I will never leave thee nor forsake thee." It is a promise which is eternal. God never leaves His children. He is with us always and will see us through anything--no matter what. What a comfort and joy it is to the person who is in the depths of despair to realize the promise he has been given. There is nothing impossible for anyone when whatever it is has been accepted in faith. It has been told to us. Can there then be any doubt that if we abide in faith it would assist us in passing through the darkest night?

I know of a family whose son was a lieutenant in the U.S. Army Reserve. I am very close to his godmother. She and his parents were extremely concerned and even alarmed when he and his unit were called to serve in Iraq. He is a young man in his early 20's with the fullness of life ahead of him. Everyone was worried about his safety and wanted him to come home unharmed. His parents and his godmother are people who are full of faith. We all agreed to pray for him every day until his return--and pray we did. We did not miss one day. Every day when I awoke to do my meditation and prayer work, I prayed for him

Many months later, when the young man returned, not only was he safe and whole, but everyone in his entire unit was unharmed. Although they had been under fire, not one person had ever been wounded or injured--such is the power of collective faith and prayer. Truly, the hope of transformation and growth starts us on our journey, but it is faith that sustains us through it. Where the journey ends is beyond both hope and faith as we move into a new day.

<u>Humor.</u> Some may think it is strange that the quality of humor may be mentioned as one of the things which can help one travel through the dark night. To my mind, it is not strange but very apparent. Throughout my life and my practice, I have seen people who have suffered devastating depression and physical hardship who have also maintained a good sense of humor. Their laughter and cheerful countenance seemed to assist them in overcoming challenges which would otherwise paralyze them. I completely agree that going through spiritual conflict and emotional upheaval is no laughing matter, but humor can be found in almost everything, and when it is, it has a tendency to help one move through the ordeal and give a different perspective.

I am reminded of a true story which I once read in the notable magazine *Readers Digest*. It was about a young woman and her ailing father. He was a man in his mid to late 60's who had contracted stomach cancer. The cancer had metastasized and was affecting his entire body. His days were numbered, and he was in terrible pain. His loving daughter visited him at the hospital as frequently as she could, expecting him to die within a few months. Her days were filled with gloom. On one visit, his stomach was extremely distended and he was very uncomfortable because, not only was he constipated due to the effects of his illness, but he was bloated and filled with gas.

At first the daughter was moved near to tears as she looked at her father's huge abdomen which was protruding from his body as he lay in the hospital bed. Suddenly, a smile crossed her face. Her father noticed and asked his daughter what was so funny. She said, "When I look at your belly, I think, why don't you bounce me on your stomach like you did when I was a little girl?" The father thought of the absurdity of the idea and they both had a hearty laugh. During the laughter, the father was able to release his gases and his stomach began to deflate. His pain subsided and he and his daughter went on to have a wonderful visit on one of his last days on earth. Humor can be found in any situation, even in the dire circumstances of a terminally ill father and a loving daughter.

Humor comes when one allows himself to be aware of his situation. As the person looks upon the panorama that is his life as it passes before him, sometimes it can seem so absurd that there is nothing to do but laugh. Even in the depths of despair, one can say, "Life is so bad, surely nothing else can go wrong," and then it does. It is at that point that one's perspective can shift from moving further into depression or into seeing the absurdity of the circumstances in which he finds himself, and rising above it to find the humor in it. The father and the daughter were able to see things from a different perspective. Their circumstances did not change, but their outlook did and it helped them to endure.

To find humor in dire situations is similar to seeing a glimmer of sunlight shining through a deep shadowy wood. The humor is a promise of the good that is to come. Even the most sorrowful spiritual aspirant can find cheer when he thinks of God's promise to him as is stated in Psalm 30:5, "In his favor is life. Weeping may endure for a night, but joy cometh in the morning." Many know of the laughing Buddha, Hotei. The character of the Buddha is based on an eccentric Chinese monk who actually lived in the Tang Dynasty over 1,000 years ago. His name was Chan'an and he was a Zen master who had such a benevolent nature and radiated such joy that he was thought to be the incarnation of the future Buddha. His laughter and humor apparently was a prelude to his enlightenment. Using humor to raise one's awareness and see a situation from a different perspective can not only give one a good laugh so that he may have a respite from his pain, but it will help him to move along the spiritual path

<u>Love.</u> There is no quality greater than love to help one through the time of desperation and despair. It is because of love, the love of God, that one sets foot on the spiritual path, and it is to go deeper into one's awareness of God which leads to contemplation and to the dark night of the soul. The very thing that brings one to the darkness is the very thing that will bring the aspirant through it. It is that which puts him on the path, keeps him on the path, and is the reward at journey's end. Persons who are enduring their spiritual quest are often cast down in depression. They are filled with self-loathing. Not only do they feel they are unworthy of God's love, they often hate themselves. One of the major tasks of psychotherapy with the depressed person is to help him with his self-esteem. As a minister, I have had a number of occasions to attend ordinations and the graduations of spiritual practitioners after they have completed a course of study. Usually, the graduates would choose an esteemed teacher who had taught their classes to speak to them as part of the ceremonies during their graduation. On one such occasion an established spiritual practitioner of many years, a distinguished African-American male in his late 50's, was chosen to address the diverse and interracially mixed class. As he was known and much respected, all of the graduates were very attentive as he came to the podium to address them. During his speech, he asked a simple question that struck a number of people present to the core. He simply asked, "Do you love yourself?" After pausing, he then said, "If you don't love yourself, how can you love God?"

It made absolute, perfect sense. Many people profess their love of the Holy Spirit and how they care for other human beings, but then do not like themselves. Being made in and out of God's own image, in order to truly love God, it follows that one must love himself. The consequence of loving oneself is that one feels good. No matter what the turmoil, when there is a glimpse of love for oneself, a beneficial emotion emerges. The essence of love has the power to overcome all of the despair. Love is the self-givingness of the Spirit and the force which harmonizes all of creation. Nothing can resist it. As the spiritual aspirant is touched by it, nothing can stay him from his course. In the soul's dark night, love pulls the seeker forward to continue. It prunes him of his many defects and impurities to make him more receptive to the love of the Divine.

One can think of how he feels when he is with someone whom he is certain loves and adores him. When a pampered child is with a loving parent, he is in his glory. He feels cherished and special. How much more so when a child of God catches a glimpse of how much God loves him. To lay in wait, through a seeming eternity, for the faintest shimmer of the light of His divine love is enough to encourage even the most disheartened. Love renews the soul and proclaims the presence of the Spirit. The promise of merging in union with the love of God keeps the seeker on his journey.

<u>Reverential Activities.</u> Overcoming the dark night of the soul is a process of purgation. The whole intent of going through the dark night is to purify the soul and purge it of impurities, false beliefs, and error. It is to purge it of its many imperfections, faults and worldly tendencies so that it may be prepared to merge into a deeper union with the Holy Spirit. There are certain practices which can help the soul on its journey. In and of themselves, they cannot take the aspirant to his destination, but they can help him along the way.

One of the practices is <u>fasting</u>. Much has been said of doing a fast. In the Bible it is mentioned that Jesus went for 40 days into the desert and fasted in order to purify himself and make himself strong enough for the great tasks which lay before him as he went about doing what he had been sent into the world to do. Fasting is more than just going without food. It is an attitude. When one is engaging in a fast, there is a turning to that which is within. It is an attempt to focus away from the needs of the body and it's attachment to the material world. The person denies himself the pleasure of tasty food and focuses on the feast of holy thoughts while concentrating on God qualities. Fasting, whether it is for a day or a month, can be extremely beneficial. It can also be extremely demanding. If not done properly, the mind goes astray and begins to think of eating "fast food" rather than concentrating on that which is sacred. It may be better for a person to fast with a group or in a secluded place, such as a monastery, so that each one can support the other in successfully completing their mission. Fasting helps because when done properly, it makes our minds more receptive to spiritual matters. Withdrawing the senses away from worldly desires helps to attune them to spiritual matters. Purging of the body through abstaining from food and completing a fast can be a spiritual victory which fortifies the soul and strengthens the will.

Another practice which helps with purgation is attending <u>retreats</u>. The great masters would go on their own individual retreat. They would go away to be alone with themselves. Buddha did it, the great saints of India, and Jesus did it as well. In fact, Buddha was in deep seclusion when he found the path to enlightenment and became awake. Most retreats, however, are not alone in a cave by oneself, or going into a deep wood to go through austerities and be renewed. Many retreats take place at a site with a group of like-minded individuals, such as a monastery, temple, or ashram. The disciples or participants go away to be alone together to engage in meditation, restricted diets, yoga, scriptural readings, and other activities so as to have their minds uplifted. Some retreats may involve simply sitting and being silent, allowing the body to slow down and remove itself from its many worldly concerns. By leaving the many distractions of his life, the aspirant is able to go within. All the activities or absence thereof of a retreat are to hasten the spiritual progress of the participants. Indeed, as they learn to go from without to within, they evolve and grow. There is an acceleration of their transformation. Also, if it is a communal retreat, the aspirant enjoys the company of the wise and kindred spirits which can be very beneficial in helping him to align himself with proper thinking in order to move through the dark night. A cleansing can take place as the person changes, however little or much, during his time in retreat.

Another very powerful practice of purgation is that of <u>forgiveness</u>. To forgive is to show love and practice positive regard for another being. We are reminded of the story in the Bible where the king brought his servant before him who had gone into great debt and owed the king ten thousand talents. Because the man could not pay, the king commanded that he be sold along with his wife, children, and all his possessions. The man fell before the king, worshipped him, and begged him to have mercy. What did the king do? He had compassion, which is borne out of love. The king forgave the man the entire debt and let him go his way. It was an act of love. The man, however, did not have a loving heart and failed to forgive a debt owed him by a fellow servant. His angry attitude and destructive actions towards his fellow servant led the king to place the debt back upon the man and it led to his undoing.

The story shows that forgiveness is borne out of love. When one forgives, he is releasing grudges, resentments and pent-up frustrations. He is letting them go so he can be more free to love. Letting go of resentments and anger is like discarding toxic emotions and impure habits. It is a cleansing. It is a purging. The person who forgives benefits as much from the act of forgiveness as the one who is forgiven. Divine forgiveness is eternal and always available. God always forgives His children, no matter what the crime. All they have to do is accept God's grace and mercy, which is always freely given. When the spiritual seeker practices forgiveness in the way of the divine nature, he is being as God is and loving as God loves. He is purged for it is written,

"To he who loves much, much is given." In his acts of compassion and forgiveness, he draws closer to God.

NOTE
1. St John of the Cross, *Dark Night of the Soul,* Image Books, New York, NY, 1990, Pg 70.

Chapter 10

Dealing With Inner Darkness

Ways and means by which the spiritual seeker accepts his own internal shadow, modifies it, and integrates it into his total being so as to be more whole as he travels the path of purgation.

The levels of the night of darkness are many. It comes to each individual according to his own experience and personal journey. When it comes, it comes in its own way to each one and to no two people does it happen in the same way. Moving through the dark night is as personal as one's relationship with God is personal. For some, it is intense, deeply moving, and profoundly purifying. For others who may be neophytes and dilettantes along the spiritual path, it may be brief, of little discomfort, and of very moderate change.

The first level of consideration would be for a person who is simply dealing with personal defects and character flaws. He or she may be depressed and want to bring about personal change. He or she may look on his imperfections as his own personal shadow. The individual may not necessarily seek to eradicate the personal defect but to resolve it or integrate it into his personality so that he may consider himself more complete. The object of someone at this level of the spiritual path is not necessarily purging but to live a better life. His efforts may be centered on simply accepting the perceived imperfection and integrating it into the totality of his own being. In fact, the particular trait may be something he may want to use. For instance, the energy he may have when he is upset may be channeled into his becoming more assertive. The aspirant may seek personal psychotherapy or spiritual counseling in order to resolve the key issues in his life. As he resolves the conflicts, he is set free of many things which restrained him from his path. There is transformation and growth. However, integrating the shadowy side of oneself is not the same as moving along the path through the dark night.

The effort of integrating the shadow brings one to a place of acceptance of his faults and helps him to either work through them or to integrate them into his life for his own personal benefit. One begins to understand his own inner darkness and integrates it into his concept of himself. The result is not necessarily spiritual transformation. In order for spiritual transformation to take place, there needs to be a purging and a changing deep within towards a greater love for God. By accepting and being aware of one's own shadow self, however, one can prepare for the true dark night of purgation and transformation.

The next level of dealing with inner darkness is the true dark night of the soul. It is associated with the purification from defects and imperfections characteristic of people who are beginners in the spiritual life. Their love of God has been awakened. There is actually a joy that they have known before they go off into the dark night. Nonetheless, they are spiritual dilettantes. They go hither and yon tasting of spiritual practices and rituals. Spiritual dilettantes enjoy the activities and are actually brought to a higher level of consciousness by their endeavors. Still, they are not truly committed to spiritual practice and have not given themselves over to God. The limitations of their practice eventually assail them and cause them grief. Instinctively, they know that it is time to go deeper spiritually. That which brought them satisfaction before no longer does. It is time to give up the sensual pleasures which they found associated with their spiritual practice. It is where many spiritual aspirants "give up the world." In order to address the profound inner darkness of the stage one has entered, it is necessary to give way to meditation and reasoning. The seeker needs to find the meaning that his journey has for him. Having delved into it, it is necessary then to accept whatever meaning has come and to pursue it actively in his life. The time for being a dilettante and tasting the many spiritual traditions is past. It is the moment to give one's life, service, and devotion completely to God.

In facing the darkness at this particular level, spiritual counseling and communities are of great value. It is helpful for the novice to develop a close relationship with a spiritual practitioner and to meet with him regularly to assist him as he travels upon his spiritual path. To go deeply into a spiritual community and chant and pray with them regularly facilitates one's personal growth. It is the occasion to enjoy the company of saints. Even at one's most morose moments, the associations can bring light. If one is diligent and practices patience and perseverance during this crucial time of transition, a purging will occur. Transformation will begin. Though there will be great pain in casting aside one's addictions and getting rid of imperfections, by being steadfast in prayer and perseverance, success is assured. The inner darkness, no matter how deep it may seem, will give way to rays of light. As the soul is rid of its addiction to sense and fleeting practices of spirit, it is transformed and becomes primed to know a deeper relationship with God. It is preparing itself for divine union with the Infinite in love.

Many aspirants, when they reach the point of preparation for a union with God, are content and desire to go no further. It is enough. They have finally reached a point where they are really living for God; why go any further? With spiritual growth achieved through their practices, meditation, patience, prayer, and all other methods which have served them well, they have journeyed through a time of personal turmoil and have overcome. However, as all seekers, especially those who have studied the new thought spiritual traditions know, the journey of transformation and spiritual growth is an endless one. There is always further evolution to be attained.

The next level of facing the inner darkness is associated with the purging of the defects of those who have advanced on the spiritual path. They are no longer neophytes. Their lives are a proven testimony to the Holy Spirit. They have suffered the trials and tribulations of the initial night of the purging of the soul from its attachment to sensual pleasures, and also, its attachment to the ways of the world. These are the ones who have been prepared to go into a deeper awareness of God and enter into preparation for lovingly merging in divine union with the Almighty. The understanding that they are one with the Holy Spirit is no longer a theoretical belief, but it is an actual experience. The experience leads the soul to pursue more purification and to take a further walk through the wilderness. The soul prepares itself, not only for the purging from sensual deficits, but also from spiritual imperfections. The ones who enter into this the darkest of nights are the ones who have dedicated their lives to God. They have been consistent in contemplating the Divine and in working on and demonstrating their faith and dedication. Often, they are people who have been engaged in decades of spiritual practice. Time, however, is not the benchmark by which they are measured but instead by their devotion and dedication to God.

In dealing with inner darkness at the more advanced level, it is necessary to be patient. It is important to persevere and pray. Reasoning and meditation can no longer help for they have brought the spiritual aspirant to the point of preparation for a deeper night of the soul, but they are not sufficient to bring the seeker through it. In fact, nothing can truly help now. In order to succeed through this important phase of the journey, the spiritual aspirant has to engage in total surrender to the will and the way of Spirit. He has to accept his pain. He has to accept whatever God gives and say, "Yes" to it. The person is actively engaged in resting in the Spirit and awaiting God's grace. It is only through intuition and spiritual insight given from on high that the rays of light are shown in this particular night. When they do come, through perseverance and patience, the aspirant needs to be readily available to accept God's grace.

I can think of one good example of someone who was on the verge of entering an advanced night of purgation. Years ago as a medical student, I took my senior break vacation by going to yoga teacher's training with the Sivanada Yoga organization at their retreat at Paradise Island in the Bahamas. It was truly a wonderful experience. We did asanas, ate vegetarian meals, and engaged in stimulating yoga practice and spiritual readings. It was designed for the purpose of teaching us to become yoga instructors and to practice a yogic life.

One of our instructors was a Western swami, a Caucasian male who was thought to be in his mid-50's. He was very vibrant and he radiated good health and energy. He was known to have been with Swami Vishnu Devananda, the founder of the yoga ashram, literally for decades. He was one of his most apt and devoted disciples. As a practitioner of yoga, he was very advanced. He knew the techniques and the reasons for them. His asanas were extremely good and his flexibility and strength was beyond that of people many years younger than he. His yearning to advance along the spiritual path was so strong that it was palpable to those around him. It was rumored around the camp that he would rise early and do many rounds of Pranayama, known as alternate nostril breathing, to elevate his energy and move himself into higher consciousness. He meditated for long periods of time and engaged in strenuous asanas, as well as teaching the classes to the new students. He was pure in his diet and chanted the holy names. He wanted desperately to advance. However, when I left the retreat he was still doing the same things and had made no movement. Years later, I learned that he was no longer a swami and had married. He continued to engage in yoga practices, but by all reports, he never went beyond the level he had attained when I first knew him. He attempted to address his yearning and desperation to come closer to God by force of will and strength of practice. It was impossible. It is only through the spirit that one can move closer to the Spirit. The aspirant has to pray, persevere, be patient, and wait in quiet receptiveness to God's call and God's light. It comes in its own time and when it comes, the seeker has to be ready and receptive, just as the wise virgins in the Bible were ready and receptive when the bridegroom arrived.

Finally, there is the ultimate, absolute darkness of the night which is experienced only by the highly evolved and most advanced along the spiritual path. It is the night which is given to the sages and the saints. The pain is so severe that no ordinary human being can endure it. Those who evolve to where they experience it are very rare. The dryness and bareness of the particular night is turmoil for the soul. It is the dark night which all spiritual masters know. There is no human remedy for it. There is no technique or practice for getting through it. Only the masters achieve it and they survive it because, as they suffer, they also have the assurance of God's hidden presence even in their pain. The evidence of His presence is the thirst that they have for God. Their longing for God is so intense that they know at some level, if the thirst for God is so strong, God must be there somewhere in his heart. Total surrender and the acceptance of the darkness with the promise of eventual union with God in love is the only way to overcome the internal turmoil.

One can think of the example of Jesus Christ. There is no greater sainted master than he. While suffering on the cross, Jesus went through a darkness and a night which no one can truly comprehend. One can only imagine the pain he felt when he was in utter darkness as he cried out in dire despair, "My God, my God, why hast Thou forsaken me?"[1] Jesus, who dwelt in the perfect knowledge of his oneness with God all the days of his life, must have been in terrible agony to feel at any moment that he was separate from the Lord. Truly, there was never a darker night for anyone. However, his surrender to and acceptance of his personal darkness was swift and sure as he then said, "Into Thy hands I commend my spirit."[2] With those words, he traversed the darkest of all nights and successfully completed his journey.

Another aspect of overcoming the dark night of the soul is works of faith. Maintaining a faith-filled perspective has been mentioned previously, but it has been said that faith without works is meaningless. One has to put his faith to use. Maintaining faith is vitally important in overcoming the dark night of the soul and works of faith are essential for its maintenance.

The work is sure to vary as one goes deeper and deeper into the wilderness of his soul. Sometimes it may be little, sometimes it may be much, or even hardly anything at all. When the journey is beyond human effort, the work is simply to keep a quiet attentiveness towards the Divine, remain at peace, and wait on God. The point is that "Faith is not a passive belief, it is a positive action."[3] It is an attitude by which one aligns himself in assurance with infinite life and possibility. To have faith is to enter into the spirit. It is to know that Spirit is. To enter into the spirit is to acknowledge and align oneself with the Spirit of God for it indeed indwells all things and all matters of spirit are one with it. When it has happened, the individual has contacted the infinite power of God and it is available to him. Although it is available, it is of no good to the person unless he decides to use it. It is the reason works of faith are important. It means the person has to make use of his faith, not sit there passively and say "I believe. I have faith," but to put it to use, and employ it to move through the shadow in which he is traversing.

Intuitively, the person will know what he has to do. Faith gives him the power and the courage to do it. As one enters into the dark night, he may have little hope, but his faith needs to be strong if he is to endure for "hope stands and waits, but faith goes to work." When the aspirant has faith, has acquired the mental attitude of a connection with the spirit, and begins to work and use the power of faith to overcome the challenges before him, his success is assured. How can it be otherwise? Having come into contact with the infinite power of the Most High, nothing can stand before him. The journey may take months, years, or even decades, but success is assured if one continues working in faith believing.

The work that is done may be individual, or it may be part of one's mission to the world. When one is going through inner turmoil, the work can be very important in keeping him focused and on his journey. Works of faith are often selfless and done in the spirit of true service. The spiritual aspirant does not seek or desire any reward. It is enough to know that he is serving God. Selfless service keeps him on the path. In fact, there is an entire spiritual tradition in the East which is dedicated to selfless service that is called Karma Yoga. It is the doing of service without attachment to result or reward. It is serving out of love for God and humanity. With Hindus in India , it is thought that when one serves with a pure heart and wants to give totally without conditions, it frees the soul from bondage and brings one liberation. Impure actions which befoul the person's life are not accumulated and do not lead to deeds from which a person must one day repent and atone. As a result, he is freed from the cycle of birth and rebirth known as reincarnation and can go on into Nirvana, self realization.

One aspect of Karma Yoga is true in all spiritual traditions. It is the giving of true service with a heart full of love that purifies the soul and prepares the mind to receive the divine light of the spirit. Works of faith are works of selfless service and bring forth purification. The nature of the work is to be an instrument of God and to do what God instructs without ego or personal agenda. No matter how great or small the task, no matter how inconsequential it may seem, if it is done in the attitude of selfless service, it is a work of faith and brings the seeker closer to God. In doing the work, gone are negative qualities of hatred and jealousy. Who has time for it? Qualities of patience, sincerity and love are developed. The soul becomes more and more pure. As the rigors of the night come upon the individual, his faith, fortified by the work he has done both internal and external, sustains him. When the work is simply to be still, he is quiet and waits in the assurance of God's love and God's grace, although the pain of the night may be severe and tortuous.

No one knows of the night while persevering and doing works of faith more than Mother Teresa, the woman who has often been called the "Saint of Calcutta India." She persevered in her mission of bringing aid to the poorest of the poor in the streets and ghettos of Calcutta, although she herself endured great personal darkness and agony as has been revealed in the book written about her life following her death. She persevered and transformed. The seeker who continues in doing works of faith and persists in his life's mission as he moves along his journey can as well.

NOTE
1. Matthew 27:4
2. Luke 24:46
3. Christian D. Larsen, *The Pathway of Roses,* Newcastle Publishing Co., Van Nuys, CA., 1994, pg 253.

Chapter 11

CASE STUDY OF THE DISABLED ADMINISTRATIVE ASSISTANT

How a single woman who was unable to work, placed on disability, and eventually fired overcame depression, grew from her ordeal, and even moved through parts of the Dark Night.

During the years I have worked in psychiatry, both as an employee and in my own private practice, I have rendered services to literally hundreds of people, many of whom were treated for depression. As a psychiatrist, most of the people that I saw were simply referrals to receive medication for their condition. However, being trained in psychoanalytic psychotherapy, I had the occasion to engage a number of people in therapy as well as give medication for their condition. Although it was not usually addressed unless the person presenting himself had a desire to do so, a number of the depressions had a spiritual component to them. In fact, several of the cases I treated would not have improved if we had not had a dialogue regarding their spiritual concerns.

Among the several cases of people with severe depression who actually experienced a transformation in the course of their treatment, one case in particular stands out. Towards the end of my practice, I had the occasion to treat an African-American woman who was one of the most depressed people I have ever seen. For purposes of convenient, I will call her Miss B. Miss B was a 42-year old, single, African-American female who had no children. She lived alone in her own apartment. At the time I saw her, she had stopped working and was receiving disability income. She was referred to me by her internist who had unsuccessfully tried to treat her with antidepressants.

At the initial interview, Miss B complained of being under emotional stress and was having problems at work. She had worked for a law firm as a paralegal and had been doing it for two years at the time of her presentation. While working there her problems began. Evidently, she was quite a capable and competent woman and was given many tasks. The more she did, the more they gave her to do. In addition to performing her duties at work, she was also going to school to become a lawyer, which was one of her dreams. As a result, she was working a demanding, full-time job while taking a challenging academic workload.

One day while at work, after being questioned on something by her own secretary, she burst into tears and cried uncontrollably. She could not stop crying. While she was in tears, she could not even catch her breath. Following the emotional outburst, she was sent home from work. She was instructed to find a doctor to find out why she had so dramatically lost control of herself. The breakdown occurred more than two months before she finally came to receive a psychiatric consultation. During the time, Miss B was profoundly depressed. Miss B's doctor had given her Zoloft, an antidepressant, to no effect. She continued to feel very badly as well as extremely lonely.

When I saw Miss B in consultation, she was experiencing severe insomnia so that she only slept three or four hours a night. As a result, she was always tired. She had no energy and no motivation to do anything. Her appetite was very poor. She was a petite woman and was in danger of losing weight. She was so depressed that every day she had a crying spell where she just sobbed for no apparent reason. She did not want to socialize or be with anybody and stayed alone, isolating herself from others. Despite her many depressive symptoms, she did not want to harm herself and there was no history of suicide attempts. Also, there was no history of any previous psychological or psychiatric problems.

Before her breakdown, Miss B was considered to be a high functioning individual and had been doing very well. At the time of her presentation, she was functioning poorly and was no longer able to work. Miss B presented as a well developed, well nourished, very attractive African-American female of light brown complexion who was of medium height and slim build. She was a petite woman, perhaps no more than 5' 4" and weighed approximately 115 pounds. Even though she was very depressed, each time she presented at my office, she was immaculately groomed. Her hair was braided or in a fashionable style and was always very neat. She wore minimal makeup which was always appropriately applied.

During Miss B's first visit, her depression was in full evidence and she cried profusely during the interview. She talked about how dismal her life had become. She had absolutely no social life and her entire existence was completely out of balance. Despite being a very pretty woman, she had no intimate relationships and had not dated or socialized in three years.

Once we began working together, I asked her about her family life. Miss B is the eldest of three children birthed by her parents. Her parents were divorced and both had remarried. Her mother went on to have two more children by Miss B's stepfather. She described a poor relationship with her mother and an even worse relationship with the stepfather who she simply called "my mother's husband."

On the other hand, she reported a very close relationship with her father who continued to call her every week, usually on a Sunday, even on into Miss B's 40's and during the time she was in therapy with me. Her father was a poorly educated laborer and a car porter. However, he was very loving towards Miss B and supported her throughout her childhood maintaining close contact with her even after his divorce from her mother. He approved of her, encouraged her, and she never doubted his love. Miss B's mother, on the other hand, was well educated. She was a registered nurse and a demanding parent who pushed

Miss B to achieve in order to win her approval. Her mother was domineering and demanding. She was also the breadwinner in the household as Miss B's stepfather was a house husband who hardly ever worked.

As treatment began in earnest, the first step that was taken was to increase Miss B's medication to make sure it was at a therapeutic level, which was done to good effect. Miss B began to have a diminishing of some of her depressive symptoms. The next step was to analyze and understand what had led to her deterioration. It was clear that her work environment was stressful and Miss B was unappreciated for her efforts. From childhood, she had a habit of trying to please demanding authority figures such as her mother. Despite Miss B's father's overwhelming approval, she still felt the need to show others that she was worthy of their respect. She denied her own happiness and well being for the sake of others--often in a way that was destructive to her welfare.

After months of abuse at work due to high demands and lack of support, the precipitating incident which triggered depression was being questioned by her secretary whom Miss B described as an older, domineering woman, probably someone much like her mother. Miss B felt unable to even stand up to the person who was supposedly working for her. She felt as if she had to please the secretary as well as everyone else.

As a result of such total self-neglect, Miss B's life became completely unbalanced. Her dream of becoming a lawyer seemed to be impossible to achieve. She lost sight of all of her goals. She felt she had no mission in life and that life was simply unfair. Once her maladaptive pattern of sacrificing her own well being and accepting overwhelming demands to please others was identified, it was presented to her to work on and to create new ways of living in the world. Although her problem was easy to identify, at first, she could not make any headway in facing it. She didn't feel worthy. She felt powerless.

Changes began to occur when she joined a church and became

an active member. One of the key moments in therapy was when she went on a women's weekend retreat with her congregation. When she returned from the retreat, Miss B appeared as happy as I had ever seen her. When asked what happened, she said she had gone on the retreat and really enjoyed it and, most importantly, she found that it was very empowering. Here was a communal experience where she was told that she had power. She was informed she is not the helpless person who she had believed herself to be. In therapy, it was emphasized that not only did she have power, but that part of her power was being able to say no to unreasonable demands, stand up for her personal rights, and use her strengths to achieve her own goals.

Miss B slowly began to take steps to move out of the darkness. Through her church and her regular activities there, she engaged in the spiritual principles of communion and fellowship with kindred spirits which were very powerful for her. In fact, she decided to give up her old friends, who she thought used her and were not supportive She would seek new friends from her church and through positive activities. Her decision was encouraged. Miss B also demonstrated the quality of trust. She trusted in God and also in the ability of the caretakers who God gave to help her.

A very key moment in therapy was when Miss B finally stood up to her mother. Her mother had used Miss B's credit cards without her knowledge and had run up a sizeable bill of several thousand dollars. Miss B was furious. After discussing the matter with me, Miss B determined her mother was in error for what she did, needed to be confronted about it, and made to correct it. I applauded Miss B's decision to confront her mother. Miss B did not allow her mother to abuse her so as to please the matriarch and instead stood up for herself. It was one of the most therapeutic moments in her treatment course. Miss B continued to exhibit other qualities which help one through the dark night such as discipline and patience. She began to exercise regularly, which can be extremely important in overcoming depression.

She used discipline to work out on a consistent basis at a local gym. Being a former high school gymnast, she responded well to the routines. The endorphins she released during her physical activities caused her to feel better. As she rounded into shape, she looked even more attractive than she had before beginning her program. Several men, both at the gym and at her church noticed. One of the gentlemen asked her out and she started to date once more.

During the many setbacks she had during therapy, she was patient with herself and persevered. In the end, Miss B overcame the worse depression and most devastating experience in her life. She went on to return to law school and obtain a law degree. During our last session when treatment was terminated, she said she was looking for a job which was not overly demanding, so that she could study for the bar while working. In one of her final declarations, she said, "I feel like a new person."

I view the treatment and experience with Miss B as being in accord with going through the dark night of the soul because there was transformation and growth. It is known that when there is a successful course of psychotherapy, often, the person will grow and be higher functioning than he was before his crisis. In fact, that is what is hoped will happen. However, in the case of Miss B, not only did she grow, but she had a transformation spontaneously recognizing it at the end of therapy. In addition, a number of spiritual activities which Miss B initiated on her own were instrumental in bringing her through her depression and darkness.

When Miss B entered her dark night, she had lost her vision. There was no hope. She saw no future for herself. She had lost her purpose in life. She viewed herself as a weak object that had to please others. After her spiritual and psychological life were awakened, she began to view herself as a being who had power and the authority to say, "No" to what she did not want. Miss B cast aside faulty perceptions and habits and acquired a greater understanding of her own sanctity and wholeness. She reclaimed her vision and declared her mission in life. When she exclaimed, "I feel like a new person," she was telling the truth. She was a new person because she had discovered who she truly is.

Chapter 12

A Brief Personal Vignette

A short account of my first experience with the darkness.

One cannot speak about moving through the darkness without touching it himself. It is personal and individual to all. I speak of the darkness because I have experienced it. It is more than a breakup with one's girlfriend, the loss of a job, or other devastating event. It hits one at his core. Also, there can be more than one dark night in an individual's life. Sometimes, it cannot be observed by the external events of a person's life because, ultimately, it is an internal struggle.

As I indicated previously, I first encountered the dark night when I was a young graduate student in Physics. At that time, I knew nothing about eventually becoming a psychiatrist. I was only 25, in excellent health and in the prime of my life.

I had a smart, red V-8 convertible, a girlfriend who loved me, a job that paid a decent salary, friends, and family. What more could a guy want? Still, I wandered around in a terrible depression. I was like the character in the Little Abner comic strip – Little Joe Btfsblk – who always had a dark cloud looming over his head to symbolize his unending bad luck. I walked around with a cloud of gloom covering me. I radiated depression. My inner world was filled with turmoil. I was lost, without vision, and saw no future worth living. My life had no meaning or purpose. I believed in God, but had no true spiritual connection. Although I have never planned a suicide attempt, on at least one occasion, I did consider it. There was no apparent reason for my depression. On the surface, everything looked good, but in truth I was deep in the dark night.

My girlfriend had grown tired of seeing me walking around in terrible agony. It was no fun for her and it was affecting our relationship. She referred me to a psychologist who served students on the campus of San Jose State University where I attended college. I entered into counseling, not knowing what to expect, but I worked hard and did not miss one session. I had a very kind mature Jewish gentleman as my therapist which was very good for me because I had very little in the way of a father figure growing up. My depression was found to be sparked by a complete absence of guidance and direction. It was grounded in seeing life as meaningless and there being no point in it. I needed to find my mission in life and a reason for living.

My therapy became a spiritual quest. In order to overcome my depression, I had to find my relation to the universe. I had to get a glimpse of the vision of my life in service to God and humanity. Of course, I worked on the conventional issues of self-esteem and correcting bad habits, as well as my relationship to my mother, but those issues paled beside the peace I had to find within myself.

We took inventory of what I valued and held most dear. I talked about my issues and even took an aptitude test. After considerable contemplation, I discovered that promoting health and peace of mind amongst humankind were some of the noblest endeavors that I thought one could attempt while living on the planet.

I considered what occupations I could enter which would most serve my values. I ultimately came up with psychiatry. A peace came over me. I felt relieved. I finally had an idea of what God wanted me to do with my life. I moved out of depression and the darkness began to dissipate. I had a glimmer of the beckoning dawn. I was in my mid-20's. I had never thought of going to medical school. Although I was making a decent amount of money, I had nowhere near what was necessary to finish medical college. I would also have to alter my academic course of study. I did not know how I would do it, but I also knew that one day I would become a psychiatrist as part of my mission on God's earth.

I had been transformed from a person who was totally lost, with no spiritual connection to the cosmos into one with a purpose and a direction. I had moved into a deeper relationship with God and had found the mission given to me by Spirit

Chapter 13

Who Is Called To The Dark

Key characteristics of all persons who are called onto the path of purgation.

There are those among us who believe that simply because they feel depressed they are in the dark night of the soul. It simply is not the truth. Depression, sad to say, is rather commonplace. If one studies psychiatric literature and reads the reports on the prevalence of depression, one will find that ten to twenty-five percent of all women, and five to twelve percent of all men, throughout the world, will experience, not brief depression, but profound depressions of significant duration at some time during their lives. Is it any wonder then that psychiatrists, psychologists, and various psychotherapists are kept busy, often becoming quite prosperous by treating the afflicted?

Despite the regularity of its occurrence, by no means is anyone ever to think that depression is normal. One is never to assume that depression is his usual condition, for in truth, the natural state of mankind is well being. Any ongoing depression will sooner or later require attention, adjustments, and often treatment. I, by no means, want to minimize the suffering of the person who is depressed, but no matter how severe his condition may be, and no matter how much pain he may be experiencing, it still may not be the dark night.

It is recommended to all people who are severely depressed to seek treatment, urgently and quickly. Many of the ways of dealing with depression have previously been discussed. There are a number of tools that may be used, and it is the task of the one who is suffering and the one helping him to find what works to bring the individual through his ordeal.

Activities which promote well being, such as exercise, even regular walking, are highly recommended. There are many therapeutic activities and they include: replacing destructive thought patterns with rational ones, changing non beneficial behaviors, using affirmations, participating in psychotherapy, and even taking medication. The prognosis for someone who truly wants to overcome his depression and is willing to work at it is quite good. However, the work which is done to become well may not involve any spiritual endeavors which is what differentiates moving through a depressive episode from that of moving from the shadows towards the light.

If one is truly in the dark night of the soul, there will be a spiritual component to what he is experiencing. It is the people who are walking along the spiritual path who enter into the wilderness known as the dark night. Not all who set foot on the spiritual path, however, enter into it. Many who begin the journey stop soon thereafter. They take their foot from the path because something else has drawn their interest. They become concerned with worldly affairs and forget about their desire for a deeper relationship with God. The ones who decide to continue on their journey eventually will encounter the night of purgation. If they persist in their spiritual practices whatever they may be - prayer, reading scriptures - whatever keeps their mind focused on the Divine, more will be demanded of them. It will not be enough to visit the temple or to go to regular Sunday services. God will urge them forth to make a deeper commitment. Spirit will send its siren call to them to cast off the role of beginners on the spiritual journey and become serious students of God's word and contemplatives of His way. Spirit is beckoning the beginners to become more. They are the ones who have been dabbling and being dilettantes in spiritual matters. They embrace meditating for awhile. Then they chant for a time. They explore reading sacred texts, such as the Bible, Koran or Bhagavad Gita for awhile. They delight in their spiritual aspirations, but commit to nothing. They may decide to embrace a tradition, such as Christianity, Islam, or Judaism, and become regular in their attendance, but remain at a surface level. God now says it is time to go deeper. It is time to find who I AM and who you really are. The spiritual aspirant may even be unconscious of the message he is receiving. Yet, there will be angst, a knowing in the gut, and a hollowness in one's being that cannot be ignored. It only becomes worse if one tries to ignore what is happening to him. The call has been sent forth. The night is beckoning. Although it is terrible, the night is also wonderful for if the spiritual aspirant chooses to travel through it, he will gain strength and cast off impurities which will set him on a straight road to a closer relationship and a deeper union with God.

Many of us like to think there is but one night and that as we traverse it, all that we will ever need to do is done and we need to embrace no more spiritual labor. It is a misconception. If one is truly called, he may enter the dark night time and time again until he completes his journey. The night may be one, but the instances may be many. The night which calls to beginners is the one of cleansing the soul of sensual impurities. It makes them ready for a more purifying night in which the soul has the spiritual aspect of itself purified as well. However, the first journey is the one which most spiritual practitioners come to and have to complete if they are to advance.

As the spiritual aspirant first encounters the dark night, he endures a purging of sensual desires and imperfections. Traits that may be evident in his character which cause him problems, such as vanity, gluttony or greed, will be exposed and he will have to work to purge himself of the traits. Bad habits which limit him and destructive tendencies which keep him embroiled in worldly conflicts and from embracing the freedom of the spirit will have to be confronted and resolved. Relationships which do not serve his spiritual journey will fall away. The spiritual aspirant will think that his world is coming apart. He is right. It is falling apart.

In my studies to become a minister, I shared classes with people who were in practitioner training to become spiritual practitioners in the principles of Science of Mind. As they became more advanced and made a firm commitment to a spiritual life, many of them went through tremendous personal upheaval. Some changed their jobs, some moved, and some even had to leave relationships. There were a few who underwent divorce. The pain they endured as they underwent the changes was tremendous. They were moving through the shadow, but they were determined to see it through to the end. Most went on to become practitioners. Some did fall by the wayside because the pain was too great, but there were a few who even went on to become ministers. What is common to all who completed the journey is that they needed a firm commitment to serving God. As one walks through the wilderness of purgation and casts off the role of dilettante on the spiritual journey, one cannot emerge from the blackness of the forest until he has given himself in service to the Lord. There has been a purging of all that would prevent the most heartfelt commitment. There has been a cleansing and the person is drawn closer to God through moving through the night of purgation.

Although nearly all spiritual aspirants who decide to remain on the path are called to the dark night of the soul, most cannot move through it, not even to the half of them. The pain is too great and the sorrows too many. As I have mentioned, I have seen it personally in my own studies with devout individuals who were pursuing their spiritual journey. Many turned back, but also more than a few did continue. All who went forward had given their lives to God and decided to give all they had in service to mankind. Many found their mission in life and had a vision of how they wanted to fulfill it. All found a closer relationship with God.

The night is terrible and its sorrows are many, but to he or she who endures to the end, the rewards are great for after completing the night of the purgation of its sensual part, the soul is converted to the service of God. It has found its reason for being. It is when the aspirant is nurtured by God. He delights in his spiritual practices. He meditates and prays regularly, sometimes for long hours. There are fasts and engagements in spiritual doctrine and tradition. There is service to others. The person grows and becomes more established in the law of the Lord.

The seeker is now no longer considered a beginner. The individual is thought to be an established person on the path, or a learned individual, or even someone who is considered to be advanced. He is someone who the 16th Century Spanish mystic, Saint John of the Cross who wrote *The Dark Night of the Soul*, would call a contemplative. He is one who seriously contemplates, dwells upon, and indulges in the ways of the spirit. He is one of the spiritual practitioners who have, to a great degree, divested themselves of worldly ways. For those who have cast aside the imperfections of the sensual part of the soul and have completed the night of sense purgation, there is yet another night.

The second dark night of the soul involves the purgation of the other part of the soul, the spiritual part. In the cleansing of the spiritual aspect of man's soul, he is then made ready for union with God in love. Simply divesting oneself of sensual imperfections is not enough. The spirit must also be made clean. The individual continues to be made pure. Even the advanced and the learned are spiritual infants before God.

Those who go into the second dark night are the highest souls. We may see them as monks or nuns of all spiritual traditions who have committed their lives totally to the spirit, so much so that they have given up all worldly things and moved to live a completely, sometimes solitary and secluded, spiritual life. Those who remain in the world daily "walk their talk" and few can find fault with them for anything. At some point, as they continue to deepen their spiritual practice, they no longer find the joy they had at first. Something again begins to call them. Despite all they have done, God wants them to go further.

Very few are the ones who enter into the second night. Very few are they who experience it. Most of us can only read about it in stories. The stories are often quite terrible and speak of great human suffering. Those who enter the spiritual night of purgation are the saints and the sages, the rare ones whom God decides to bring even closer to Him and His love.

The Bible speaks of a deep, dark night in the book of Job. Job was upright before the Lord. He feared God and shunned evil. For his steadfastness, he was blessed. He had thousands of sheep and hundreds of cattle. He had great wealth, seven sons and three daughters. He engaged in daily spiritual practices and honored God. The Lord said of Job that there was none like him on the earth, a perfect and upright man. Yet, he was cast into trials and tribulation. He entered into a terrible darkness. All of his cattle and sheep were taken from him. His great wealth was destroyed. He even lost his sons and daughters who were killed in a great tragedy.

Job mourned his losses and suffered greatly. His body was afflicted with boils, and he was wracked with pain. His friends could not comfort him or give him insight as to his suffering. It was only when God came and spoke to him that he found wisdom and felt relief. Though Job was perfect in many ways, his spirit was still in need of cleansing for Job lacked humility. He knew of his uprightness and bemoaned his suffering as being unjust. God came to Job and let him know that there are none who are righteous before the Lord. There are none who can decide whether God is just in his judgment. When Job realized his error, he was cleansed. He repented and surrendered to God. He clothed himself in humility. On completing his great night of purgation, Job was blessed more greatly than before with more cattle, oxen, and sheep, seven more sons and three more daughters more beautiful than the ones he had lost. More importantly, he had a deeper, closer relationship with God than he had ever had previously. The darkness had purged Job's spirit and brought him into a closer relationship with God.

We see that there can be more than one night of darkness and purification. Ernest Holmes, the founder of Science of Mind, tells us that we are on an ongoing spiritual journey which is an eternal upward spiral. Essentially, it means that we are always growing spiritually. We are always finding opportunities to evolve as spiritual beings. The occasion may present itself as a black period, a time of living in the shadow. There may be more than one night of trial in our lives to strengthen us and purify us. There may be times we do not understand it or why it is happening. Also, for the saints and sages, no human effort can bring them through it. They have to attune themselves in quietude and attentiveness to God. Only by being in alignment with the Holy Spirit can one move into divine union with God as the nights of purgation of the spirit are endured.

As has been said, the great vast majority of humankind need not worry about the night of purging of the spiritual part of the soul, for although we all have the potential, we probably are not going to become that pure and righteous. I am reminded of the TV commercial, "The few, the proud, the Marines." On the spiritual journey, it can be reworded as "the rare, the humble, the Saints." They and those who are evolved like them are the only ones who need worry about or concern themselves with the second night of the purgation of the soul's spiritual essence.

Although we may not attain the lofty heights, we can be inspired by those who do. There is no doubt in my mind that the author of the poem and book *Dark Night of the Soul*, Saint John of the Cross himself, endured a rather lengthy and very painful night of darkness which enabled him to give to the world a great work which has lasted for centuries and has touched millions. Due to his spiritual evolution, he was able to speak from personal experience on all levels of spiritual purging and cleansing.

During the 20th Century, there has been another who has inspired us to persevere by her example. It is the woman commonly referred to as Mother Teresa, who has come to be known as the Saint of Calcutta. Her dedication to serving the extreme poor on the streets of Calcutta is legendary. Her image around the world prior to her death was always one of assurance. She was calm and dedicated. She led the sisters of her order with love and caring. Only a select few people in the entire world knew that she suffered long periods of darkness and spiritual turmoil. After her passing, a book composed of her letters to her closest spiritual directors entitled *Come Be My Light* was printed which detailed her suffering. She explained that it all began on September 10, 1946 as she rode on a train traveling to Darjeeling, India. During the ride, she received a call from God. It was a mystical encounter with Christ. She heard a call to give up everything and follow Him into the slums. She was to serve Christ amidst the poorest of the poor. Prior to her call, Mother Teresa had been extremely happy. She enjoyed her life as a nun and the work that she did. She felt a union with God. However, the call she received was a message to go deeper and as she began her mission to be a light to those who dwelled in darkness, she began to experience the darkness.

In Mother Teresa's letters to her spiritual directors, she spoke of the terrible pain she felt. She described an untold darkness, a profound loneliness, and a continual longing for God. It produced a painful agony deep within her heart. Sometimes, she felt there was no God in her soul, that she was blank and God was completely absent from her. For someone who had closely felt an intimate connection with Spirit, nothing could cause more agony and suffering. Even while she was doing her great works, she felt the inner pain. It seemed to be a part of her. She just longed for God and thought that God did not want her.

During her mission, Mother Teresa dealt with the intense distress which she felt within herself. She was able to live through her pain by giving total surrender to Christ and placing a loving trust in Him. In her acceptance of the darkness and surrender to the will of God, she said "Yes" to the Holy Spirit and allowed herself to be used by Him as a vehicle through which He did His holy work.

Still, in moments of great agony, Mother Teresa attempted to understand why she was in such darkness. What was the reason she was experiencing so much spiritual dryness? Why was she suffering? In her search and in her communications with her spiritual directors, it finally came to light that her darkness, though similar to the dark night of the soul, was not quite the same. The defect of even many of the most advanced spiritual practitioners was not in her. The darkness served to help her share in the passion of Jesus and in his suffering. In so doing, it made her feel a closer bond and union to Him. Also, most importantly, her inner darkness gave her the ability to understand the feelings of the poor on an intimate level. When she understood the reasons for her bleak experiences, she came to say that she loved the darkness. She endured the pain for the strength and the love that it ultimately inspired in her.

Among the sages and saints who have walked the earth, Mother Teresa is but one who has suffered in the darkness. In truth, the dark night of the soul is something which all masters of spiritual life know or will know. It was true of even the greatest of the saints and sages, Jesus the Christ – the Master Teacher, and the Buddha himself. Jesus the Christ experienced it while dying on the cross at Calvary when he felt abandoned by his Father. Jesus had made the profound statement that "I and my Father are one."[1] He lived in that truth, yet he had a moment of terrible blackness when he did not experience the Father. However, because he had absolute knowledge of whom and what he is, the moment was fleeting. The very next instant, Jesus traversed the dark night and embraced God in sweet surrender as he took his last breath and commended his spirit into the hands of the Holy Spirit.

Buddha, the Awakened One, also went through the dark night. When he sat on the banks of the river underneath the Bodhi tree, he decided that he would not rise again until he was enlightened. His pain was so great at trying to find truth and to overcome the ignorance of the world that he had determined that he would rather die than continue as he had. He was deep in the dark night. It is said that his was an intense and incomparable struggle as he sat on the banks of the river. Some say it was only a night. Others say it was longer, perhaps even weeks. During the time he sat, his blood ran thin, his flesh and his bones cracked. However, he endured. When he arose in the morning, his mind was clear, and he had found the path to enlightenment.

If all spiritual masters must transcend the dark night of the soul, how much more must it be true of we who are aspiring to be nearly as good as they and seek to know the joy that they have known. The dark night of the soul is no stranger to any who truly seek to know God and find divine union in God's love.

NOTE
1. JOHN 11:30

Chapter 14

COMPLETING THE JOURNEY

Signs, lessons, and benefits which demonstrate that the spiritual aspirant is finishing his period of purging and moving into the light for the reward at journey's end.

For he who completes the journey from the shadow and through the darkness into the divine light of enlightenment and God's love, there are many blessings. He or she has achieved a great victory, and there is spiritual sweetness to be had. There is reward even in completing the smallest part of the journey, but to one who endures the tortures of the night of purging to the end and goes from a beginner on the spiritual path to one who is proficient, the rewards are great. They may or may not be seen outwardly; still, the inner life becomes rich and meaningful.

The journey from the shadow has often been like traveling through a vast wilderness. In the depths of the forest, there appears to lurk many terrors and dangerous beasts. Many are the ones who turn back and do not continue upon the journey. As has been said, not even half of those who begin the journey complete it. The horrors which are encountered afflict the mind, the body, and the heart. The soul suffers grievously. Some will stay the course and steadily trek through the deadly wood. Others may stop there for awhile, if they should find a safe haven, and rest before continuing their journey. They are the ones who enter the night but find respite for a while until finding the strength to continue. Such is the spiritual path and the walk through the dark night. One must be ever diligent of the dangers that assail one's spirit and not give in to doubt, fear or discouragement but maintain faith and perseverance. All the seeming obstacles will be overcome much as the faith of a mustard seed that moves the mighty mountain.

What the aspirant needs to remember is that he has been chosen. God has drawn him forth. Infinite Intelligence no longer wants him to be simply a beginner, but wants the person to become proficient in the ways of the spirit, to become more advanced in the practices of the spiritual life and come into a closer relationship with Him. God wants the aspirant to succeed. It is one of the reasons he completes his journey. The call from Spirit has drawn him forth to leave the role of beginner and dilettante and become committed to a spiritual life. The trials of the dark night are to purge and cleanse him, make him ready for a new way of living, and to prepare him to be more receptive to God's divine love.

As one completes the journey, there are signs that one is near its end. One such sign is that a person who previously had no purpose in life suddenly finds that he or she has one. He has discovered a calling, something which God has told him to do as he listens to the inner voice. The call is unique and personal to each and every one according to his abilities and understanding. It may be something that is great in the eyes of the world, or it can be exceedingly humble. However, it is the aspirant's calling. Perhaps it is to feed the homeless. It could be working in a nursery serving children. It could be entering the ministry, becoming a lawyer to the defenseless, or a doctor to serve the physically ill. The calls are many. What is important is that something which the person had not heard before draws him to a commitment of giving to humankind and of service to God, as it has manifested in him. The true sign of completing the journey is having a mission in life where there was none before and becoming a place of service to God and man. Absolute Love, the Holy Spirit, gives completely of Itself. Spiritual seekers who complete the journey are like unto the Spirit and give of themselves.

A well-known minister, Reverend Doctor Michael Beckwith, who is the founder and senior minister of the Agape International Center of Truth, a Transdenominational Ministry in Culver City, California, is fond of saying, "You are to become a beneficial presence on the planet." When one completes the journey through the first night of purgation and divests himself of much of his sensual defects of the soul he does become a beneficial presence on the Earth. He or she is known, as it is said in the Bible, by his love and how he loves others. He gives of himself in selfless service, often seeking nothing for himself and dedicating it all to God. If one is doing his best to complete his journey through the dark night, it would be well advised to begin giving, to visualize his mission, and to commit himself to a spiritual life in service to God. It will help him to pass through the darkness.

As previously mentioned, depression is a part of the dark night of the soul. Sometimes it appears that those who suffer severe depressions believe they are in the dark night when indeed they are not. Nonetheless, it is necessary to overcome depression to truly leave the shadow behind.

As one continues in patience and perseverance to walk in the direction of his final goal, the trappings of depression will begin to fall away. Old habits which cause heartache are shown to be the imperfections of the sensual part of the soul. They are the habits that limit one's progress and keep him in continual suffering. The doubts, fears, and misguided thinking are illuminated as one deals with the depression. As the cleansing and purging comes, be it through psychotherapy, spiritual counseling, medication, support groups, personal practice, or whatever else it may be, new habits are acquired. Correct and positive thinking replace misguided conceptions and assumptions. The mind is renewed and, as the mind is renewed, life is renewed.

Often, if one has worked through a crisis, be it interpersonal or of a spiritual nature, he emerges stronger than he ever was before the crisis. New ways of living and being in the world have been learned and the person functions at a higher level than previously--sometimes beyond his own imaginings. It is the benefit of overcoming depression through diligent work, whether it is in coping with depression alone, or in association with the dark night. What counts is that there is a change in terms of the person's well being. There is higher functioning. The changes in habits and thoughts lead to a better life and a better way of handling challenges which arise in one's life.

In overcoming depression and moving into a higher state of being, it is important to remember that help comes from all sources, and one must be willing to accept it as it comes. It is the natural state to feel good and to be able to contribute to both self and others. When in the depths of depression, it is wise to remember that "this too shall pass." The prognosis is good and very good. If the depression is part of the dark night, God wants you to come through it. Your success is assured. If it is not a part of the dark night, all health indicators show that the odds are in favor of the person who is suffering. He needs to continue to seek the necessary help to ensure his success. There will be progressive changes in his state of well being. It may take weeks or even months, but soon, there will be a new way of life and, at the end of the journey, all will be well.

As the dark night of the soul is chiefly concerned with the purging of imperfections to make the soul ready for a more loving relationship with God, spiritual benefits are a necessary part of the completion of the journey. As he nears the journey's end, the spiritual aspirant will gain new insight about himself and his spiritual practice.

Therefore, one gift of the night is that of increased self knowledge. The spiritual seeker has been in such pain through becoming aware of deficits and imperfections in character and habits that he is no longer filled with pride. He loses much of his ego. He sees his faults, but fortunately, God shows him his strengths, too. The person utilizes the knowledge to help him continue his journey. It has been said, "Know thyself," and that is exactly what happens in the course of walking through the shadow. With a more intimate knowledge of himself and the misery that he has endured, the seeker is better able to cast aside ego and move into a deeper union with God. As a consequence of the self-knowledge, he is now more able to move into communion with the Divine. There is a connection with God perceived at a deeper level than ever before. The imperfections which presented in the past have been eradicated and, with his new-found humility, the traveler approaches God with more respect and reverence than previously, which is pleasing to God, and it helps him to move forward along his spiritual path. The humility and reverence which the person has learned gives him an attitude which allows him to gain more knowledge of spiritual matters and, in addition, God gives unto him more knowledge of Himself. The humility and self knowledge that has been gained through the night is of great benefit to the one who has persevered.

Another benefit is that of love for one's neighbor. When one has suffered and felt persecuted in the dark night and has borne many afflictions, there is a tendency thereafter to be kinder, not only towards oneself, but also towards others. One feels more compassion for all people, and in fact, for all beings.

I am reminded of the time when I was going through a period of darkness following the death of my mother. The proceedings surrounding her death were very unpleasant for me and haunt me even to this day. A short while after my mother's passing, I was seeing the older Jewish woman to whom I referred earlier. She was experiencing the terminal illness of her son, who was dying of cancer. She felt hopeless, persecuted, and alone. I sat with her as she spoke of her immense pain over the prospect of losing her loved one. As we talked, I recalled the agony I felt during my mother's illness and subsequent transition. I was able to connect with and understand her in a way I never had previously. I was overwhelmed with compassion for her and felt a strong sense of love which nearly brought us both to tears. She felt comforted and reassured freely releasing her pent up emotions. The love and compassion that I had been able to gain in my own suffering had extended to feelings of love and understanding towards her as my neighbor and fellow traveler moving through the dark night in addition to strengthening our therapeutic alliance. The compassion one develops for one's own self allows him to have more compassion for others. Also, the caring and acceptance one has to find in order to survive the dark night is of spiritual benefit and further helps in the loving of self and all being.

As a person moves through the dark night and reaches its end, one of the consequences is that he leaves behind the role of beginner and becomes more practiced and proficient in the ways of the spirit. It is a great benefit which assists him in beginning to cultivate virtues. In traveling through the wilderness, many of the virtues may already have been established, one of them being patience. There are those on the path who make rapid progress and who move through their trials quickly. However, many people have to persist for years and even decades in order to complete their journey. During the time, there may be periods of light. God will give the seeker glimpses of His love, so that he will be encouraged to continue and to not lose heart. Yet, the glimmer of light and the radiance of His love will be followed by more darkness. The journey goes on and the seeker continues to walk along his path. It is then when patience is truly a virtue. Just to continue to trod through the shadow is to acquire patience, a virtue which is of great benefit to anyone in all areas of life.

The seeker also acquires charity. In completing the night, he has learned that Spirit is giving and in order to be like Spirit one has to give. The seeker is now more charitable to himself and his fellow man. He gives, often seeking nothing in return, and dedicates his works to God. He does not seek to be praised for his generous spirit. Instead, he seeks to give as much as he can out of the love that he has gained.

Many other virtues are often acquired along the way such as courage and fortitude, for it takes both in order to continue. It takes courage to face ones doubts and fears; one of the virtues that one acquires in completing the night as he overcomes his challenges and faces the things which frighten him the most.

A great benefit is an increase in faith. Faith is necessary for an aspirant to continue on the journey. However, the completion of the journey is such a powerful demonstration that one's faith is increased. It becomes the faith to move mountains. The eyes are uplifted. The soul is elevated and one can see possibilities. Doubt limits a person, but faith sets him free. The person casts aside what he previously believed was impossible for him to do and removes the restrictions placed upon his life that had not yet been overcome. The person is finally free to see endless possibilities knowing that through faith it can be provided for him. He now has the power to achieve his potential. If he has the vision, he can accomplish what he desires. There is, in many ways, no greater spiritual benefit.

There is also an eradication of many worldly desires. In completing the dark night of the soul, many of the sensual parts are cleansed. It is necessary in order to make one ready for living a divine life. The seeker is less likely to "backslide." Desires and temptations which once led him astray no longer have power over him. His heart longs more for that which personifies spiritual living. He is more able to lead a virtuous life. The purging has set him free. Habits, thoughts, people, and conditions which previously held him prisoner and caused him to have experiences which led him to suffer no longer have power over him. The spiritual seeker is free. It is said that he who is free in the spirit is free indeed. By virtue of the purging of the dark night, the spiritual seeker is now considered to live in and by Spirit. He may or may not be able to do it completely, for very few are able to complete the cleansing of the spiritual part of the soul; they are the saints and sages of whom there are very, very few. Nonetheless, by purging himself of the sensual parts of his nature, the spiritual seeker is essentially living in the spirit and has the liberty that accompanies it.

The blessings which accompany the spiritual aspirant when finishing the journey also include the return of the sweetness that the person enjoyed as a beginner before he entered the dark night; however, it is even more so than before the journey was begun. Due to what he has endured, there is an inner peace and an increase in wisdom in all spiritual understanding. The joy he now experiences is greater than ever before because he is not rejoicing in the artifacts of the spirit, but his joy is in the Lord, in serving God, and in contemplating matters of the Spirit. The one who has completed the journey finds fullness of joy.

Another part of completing the journey is transformation. The person who started the journey is not the same one who finishes it. There has been transformation. The person has grown and become more adept within himself and in spiritual matters. He is better able to enter into a deeper, loving relationship with life and, most of all, with the Infinite.

In many ways, the person who began the journey was like a child in the spirit. He began with rough tools. He was pleased with the pleasures allowed to him by Spirit as he began his quest. However, as he continued along on his spiritual journey more was demanded of him. He could no longer play at the matters of spirit as if they were toys. Spiritual matters are serious for they involve one's life and his relationship with the universe. After a time, it is no longer appropriate to be a dilettante. One must make a commitment. God pulls the person forth and away from the ways of children, tells him to put away his toys, and draws him into the dark night, so that he may be tempered, strengthened and nourished to become a man or woman of God. He is transformed from the state of being like unto a child and evolves into an adult of the Spirit. He goes from beginner to proficient and, further still, becomes one who is advanced in the ways of the Lord.

Although the great majority of us do not attain it, despite the fact that we all have the potential, there are a precious few who are moved even into enlightenment. They are the ones who are the saints and the sages who are transformed beyond the mortal sphere. Even when they are with us, their dark night is so profound and mystical as to be beyond our understanding. Their transformation is beyond that of going from a child in the spirit into coming to be an evolved adult; it is into becoming a being who is beyond our human understanding. They can be understood only through the grace and the will of God.

All who are transformed are also converted into the service of God. Many think that it is there where the journey ends and that there is nothing more. However, the founder of Science of Mind, Dr. Ernest Holmes, said: "There is more to us than we realize. Man is an eternal destiny, a forever-expanding principle of conscious intelligence."[1] Thus, we are eternally evolving into higher aspects of the Spirit and the realms of life. The journey, though thought to be complete for a time, is one of ongoing spiritual growth and evolution.

Yes, the passage from the shadow into the light is an onerous one ripe with trials and tribulation. The purging and cleansing are associated with both spirituality and suffering. Removal of deficits and imperfections are associated with pain, deep despair, depression, and agony. Yet, the joys and rewards are profound and far outweigh what one has to suffer to obtain them. The evolution which takes place in one's spirit and very soul as he travels through the darkness brings him into preparation for a deep union with God in love. There can be no greater prize to be had. Moving from the shadow into the light through the dark night of the soul is likened to going from the twilight of the evening to the breaking of the dawn. It is a time when the perceived light dims until there is total darkness causing one to believe that all is lost. However, within the bleakness, one continues the journey. Then, there is the breaking dawn, the glimpse of the sun which is rising on the horizon. It is the light and love of God which has broken through into the consciousness of the one who has been seeking It.

NOTE

1. Ernest Holmes, *The Science of Mind,* Penguin Putnam, Inc. New York, NY, 1938, pg 288

BIBLIOGRAPHY

Aaron T. Beck, M.D., <u>Cognitive Therapy and the Emotion Disorders</u>, Penguin Books, USA, Inc., New York, NY, 1979.

Deepak Chopra, <u>The Seven Spiritual Laws of Success</u>, Amber-Allen Publishing San Rafael, CA. and New World Library Novato, CA, 1994.

John F. Cooper, <u>A Primer of Brief Psychotherapy</u>, W. W. Norton & Company Co., New York, NY, 1995.

St. John of the Cross, <u>Dark Night of the Soul</u>, translated and edited by E. Allison Peers, Image Books, New York, NY, 1990.

Ram Dass, <u>Journey of Awakening</u>, Banton Books, New York, NY, 1978.

Divine revelation through the Prophet Muhammad, <u>The Koran</u> with a parallel Arabic text, Translated with notes be N.J. Dawood, Penguin Books, Ltd., 1995.

Swami Vishnu Devananda, <u>Mediation and Mantras</u>, OM Lotus Publishing Co., New York, NY, 1981.

Robert S. Ellwood, <u>Many Peoples, Many Faiths</u>, Fifth edition, Prentice-Hall, Inc., Upper Saddle River, New Jersey, 1996.

Erik H. Erikson, <u>Childhood and Society</u>, Second edition, W. W. Norton & Company, Inc., New York, NY, 1963.

Charles Filmore, <u>Metaphysical Bible Dictionary</u>, fourteenth printing, Unity Books, Unity Village, Missouri, 2000.

Debbie Ford, <u>The Dark Side of the Light Chasers</u>, Riverhead Books, New York, NY, 1998.

Kahil Gibran, <u>The Prophet</u>, Seventy-second printing, A Borzol Book published by Alfred A. Knopp, Inc., New York, NY, 1965.

Joel S. Goldsmith, <u>Consciousness is What I Am</u>, edited by Lorraine Sinkler, I-level Publications, Austell, Georgia, 1976.

Ernest Holmes, <u>Living the Science of Mind</u>, DeVorss & Company, Publisher, Publisher, Camarillo, CA, 1984.

Ernest Holmes, <u>The Science of Mind</u>, Penguin Putnam, Inc., New York, NY, 1938.

Philip G. Janicak, M.D., John M. Davis, M.D., Sheldon H. Preskorn, M.D., Frank J. Ayd, Jr., M.D., Stephen R. Marden, M.D., and Mani N. Pavuluri, M.D., Ph.D., <u>Principles and Practice of Psychopharmacotherapy</u>, Fourth edition, Lippincott Williams & Wilkins, a Wolters Kluwer business, Philadelphia, PA, 2006.

Carl Jung, <u>Modern Man in Search of a Soul</u>, translated by W.S. Dell and Gary F. Baynes. Harvest/HBJ Books Harcourt Brace Jovanovich New York, NY and London, England, 1933.

Harold I. Kaplan, M.D. and Benjamin J. Sadock, M.D., <u>Synopsis of Psychiatry, Behavioral Sciences/Clinical Psychiatry</u>, Eighth edition, Williams & Wilkins, Baltimore, Maryland, 1998.

Bukkyo Dendo Kyokai (Buddhism Promoting Foundation), <u>The Teaching of Buddha</u>, Fifteenth edition, Kenkyusha Printing Co., Tokyo, Japan, 1971.

Christian D. Larsen, <u>The Pathway of Roses</u>, Newcastle Publishing Co., Inc. Van Nuys, CA., 1994.

Peter Sifneos, M.D., <u>Short-Term Psychotherapy and Emotional Crisis</u>, Harvard University Press, Cambridge, Massachusetts, 1972.

Sri Swami Sivananda, <u>Sure Ways for Success in Life and God-Realization</u>, The Divine Life Society, U.P., Himalayas, India, 1970.

Donna M. Sudak, M.D., <u>Cognitive Behavioral Therapy for Clinicians</u>, Lippincott, Williams & Wilkins, a Wolters Kluwer business, Philadelphia, Pennsylvania, 2006.

Mother Teresa, <u>Come Be My Light</u>, edited and with commentary by Brian Kolodiejchuk, M.C., Doubleday Broadway Publishing Group, a division of Random House, Inc., New York, NY, 2007.

Task Force on DMS-IV, <u>Diagnostic and Statistical Manual of Mental Disorders</u>, Fourth edition, American Psychiatric Association, Washington, D.C., 1994.

The Holy Bible, King James Version, Thomas Nelson Publishers, Nashville, Tennessee, 1976.

Trungpa, Chogyam, Meditation In Action, Shambhala Publications, Inc., Boston Massachusetts,1996.

ABOUT THE AUTHOR

Reverend Dr. Herman Brooks graduated from Howard University School of Medicine in Washington, D.C. in 1978. He went on to complete a residency in psychiatry at Sepulveda V. A. Medical Center, an affiliate of UCLA, which is located in San Fernando Valley, California.

After finishing his course of study, he worked as a community psychiatrist performing both inpatient and outpatient service for Augustus F. Hawkins Mental Health Hospital and outpatient treatment for Kedren Mental Health Clinic both facilities being located in South Central Los Angeles. While working, he studied for and obtained his Diplomat of the American Board of Psychiatry and Neurology in 1985.

Reverend Dr. Brooks continued to serve in clinical settings until deciding to establish his own private practice in 1990. His psychiatric specialization included: psychotherapy, psychopharmacology, and, when necessary, hospitalization. During the time that he served in the Los Angeles clinics, he became appalled at the disregard for life which seemed to be apparent in many of the tragic losses suffered by a number of his patients. Many of the families had lost loved ones to senseless, random violence as in drive-by shootings and violent assaults. It was during that time when he had an epiphany after reading an article in *The Los Angeles Times* about a beloved priest in the Boyle Heights area who was leaving his parish. The area was full of gang violence, and he had attempted to stop it by simply loving the parishioners so much that they would stop harming others. It hit Dr. Brooks that the priest's idea could never work, but that the people would have to love themselves in order to change. He then resolved to use all he had learned spiritually and psychologically to show individuals in the community who they truly are; divine and sacred beings who are the beloved of God. It is in the moment of awakening when people embrace the truth that they will begin to change and begin to treat one another with love. Following the epiphany, he received his "call" to the ministry when it occurred to him to be a center of consciousness to spread the truth of the One Love and One Life of all in God, and to affirm the sacredness of the life of all people. It becomes imperative to know the truth of the preciousness of one's life and the lives of others. Once acknowledged and accepted, one must bring about change in himself and in his community.

Through a fortunate coincidence, he discovered Agape International Center of Truth, a New Thought Transdenominational Spiritual Center which at the time was part of the United Church of Religious Science. He was inspired by the founder and senior minister, Reverend Dr. Michael Beckwith. It was the experience which led him to embrace the teachings of Religious Science and to enter the Holmes Institute School of Ministry. He viewed principles he learned as being the vehicles by which he could spread the truth of the sacredness of life and the communion of the Spirit in all. He eagerly plunged into his course work and graduated from the school of ministry in 2001.

After taking a brief break, he received a letter of call to the Ahiah Center for Spiritual Awakening in Pasadena, California. There he served under the Reverend Charles Roses and eventually satisfied the requirements to be ordained, a ceremony which took place in September, 2005.

Although he closed his private practice in 2004, he continues to work as a psychiatric consultant for two clinics in the Los Angeles area. Since his ordination, however, he has been actively visioning and working to establish a ministry which will enable him to answer the call he has been given to spread the message of One Love and the sacredness of each and every life. He has previously had an article about anxiety entitled "Be Blessed, Not Stressed" published in the September 2002 issue of Science of Mind magazine. The book, <u>Making it Through the Dark Night of the Soul</u>, a thesis on depression and transformation, is his first major work and heralds his unfolding vision as he goes about fulfilling the mission he has accepted.